Database Replication

Synthesis Lectures on Data Management

Editor

M. Tamer Özsu, *University of Waterloo*

Synthesis Lectures on Data Management is edited by Tamer Özsu of the University of Waterloo. The series will publish 50- to 125 page publications on topics pertaining to data management. The scope will largely follow the purview of premier information and computer science conferences, such as ACM SIGMOD, VLDB, ICDE, PODS, ICDT, and ACM KDD. Potential topics include, but not are limited to: query languages, database system architectures, transaction management, data warehousing, XML and databases, data stream systems, wide scale data distribution, multimedia data management, data mining, and related subjects.

Database Replication
Bettina Kemme, Ricardo Jiménez Peris, and Marta Patiño-Martínez
2010

User-Centered Data Management
Tiziana Catarci, Alan Dix, Stephen Kimani, and Giuseppe Santucci
2010

Data Stream Management
Lukasz Golab and M. Tamer Özsu
2010

Access Control in Data Management Systems
Elena Ferrari
2010

An Introduction to Duplicate Detection
Felix Naumann and Melanie Herschel
2010

Privacy-Preserving Data Publishing: An Overview
Raymond Chi-Wing Wong and Ada Wai-Chee Fu
2010

Keyword Search in Databases
Jeffrey Xu Yu, Lu Qin, and Lijun Chang
2009

Database Replication

Bettina Kemme, Ricardo Jiménez Peris, and Marta Patiño-Martínez

ISBN: 978-3-031-00711-8   paperback
ISBN: 978-3-031-01839-8   ebook

DOI 10.1007/978-3-031-01839-8

A Publication in the Springer series
SYNTHESIS LECTURES ON DATA MANAGEMENT

Lecture #7
Series Editor: M. Tamer Özsu, *University of Waterloo*
Series ISSN
Synthesis Lectures on Data Management
Print 2153-5418   Electronic 2153-5426

Database Replication

Bettina Kemme
McGill University

Ricardo Jiménez Peris
Technical University of Madrid

Marta Patiño-Martínez
Technical University of Madrid

SYNTHESIS LECTURES ON DATA MANAGEMENT #7

ABSTRACT

Database replication is widely used for fault-tolerance, scalability and performance. The failure of one database replica does not stop the system from working as available replicas can take over the tasks of the failed replica. Scalability can be achieved by distributing the load across all replicas, and adding new replicas should the load increase. Finally, database replication can provide fast local access, even if clients are geographically distributed clients, if data copies are located close to clients.

Despite its advantages, replication is not a straightforward technique to apply, and there are many hurdles to overcome. At the forefront is replica control: assuring that data copies remain consistent when updates occur. There exist many alternatives in regard to where updates can occur and when changes are propagated to data copies, how changes are applied, where the replication tool is located, etc. A particular challenge is to combine replica control with transaction management as it requires several operations to be treated as a single logical unit, and it provides atomicity, consistency, isolation and durability across the replicated system. The book provides a categorization of replica control mechanisms, presents several replica and concurrency control mechanisms in detail, and discusses many of the issues that arise when such solutions need to be implemented within or on top of relational database systems.

Furthermore, the book presents the tasks that are needed to build a fault-tolerant replication solution, provides an overview of load-balancing strategies that allow load to be equally distributed across all replicas, and introduces the concept of self-provisioning that allows the replicated system to dynamically decide on the number of replicas that are needed to handle the current load. As performance evaluation is a crucial aspect when developing a replication tool, the book presents an analytical model of the scalability potential of various replication solution.

For readers that are only interested in getting a good overview of the challenges of database replication and the general mechanisms of how to implement replication solutions, we recommend to read Chapters 1 to 4. For readers that want to get a more complete picture and a discussion of advanced issues, we further recommend the Chapters 5, 8, 9 and 10. Finally, Chapters 6 and 7 are of interest for those who want get familiar with thorough algorithm design and correctness reasoning.

KEYWORDS

database replication, transactions, replica control, 1-copy-equivalence, consistency, scalability, fault-tolerance, performance, elasticity

To Maya and Sophia

Bettina

To my parents Ricardo and Maria Adelina,
my siblings David and Ana, and my son Alejandro

Ricardo

To my parents Manuel and Cele,
my brother Manolo, and my son Alejandro

Marta

Contents

CHAPTER 1

Overview

1.1 MOTIVATION

Many business services have gone online. For instance, online banking and online shopping have become standard activities in our daily lives, and we expect a smooth user experience. The services need to be available around the clock, and respond within seconds – whether there are many thousands of users accessing the system at the same time or one is the only person in the world using it. How do the service providers achieve this? In fact, they use the same principle that was applied in the old times: replication. A generation ago, when banking and shopping were still tasks that forced you to leave your home, when still real people were in charge of serving your requests, replication was standard practice. The more customers lived in an area and demanded the service, the more bank clerks and cashiers were hired. Backups were on call should the main staff become sick. Now, compute nodes[1] replace the human beings. Service execution is distributed over all nodes. If the number of users increases, more nodes are added to share the load, guaranteeing that the quality of service remains acceptable. If a node fails, a failover procedure transfers the tasks executing on the failed node onto another node, making the failure imperceptible to the end user.

Replication is relatively straightforward if a service only requires computation but has no critical data or information associated with it, i.e., the service is stateless. However, many services are stateful, meaning they use and manipulate business critical data such as money transfers of a bank client or purchase information in a bookstore. Such data are typically stored in a database system. Then, coordination among nodes becomes more challenging. In fact, in many cases, not only the service functionality is replicated but also the data so that each node can access its own copy of the data. Informally, database replication means that the logical data items of the database (e.g., the tuples in a relational database or the objects in the object-oriented world) have multiple physical copies, located on different nodes. Database replication is precisely the topic of this book.

Database replication is used by many different applications, not only banking and e-commerce. It is used for many different purposes and deployed over a range of computer configurations. It can be small- or large-scale, affecting a few data items or terabytes of data. Obviously, given the diversity of applications and environments, there is no one-fits-all replication solution. Instead, a replication approach has to consider many different issues and must be specifically designed and adjusted to the particular task on hand.

---

[1]A node could mean many things. In this book, node mostly refers to a physical machine. But it could also be a virtual machine running on a physical computer, e.g., in the cloud.

Figure 1.1: Fault-tolerance architecture

Let us have a closer look at a replication solution. For better illustration, we use the example of an online store selling some products, say puppets. The store's web site offers functionality to query the catalogue of puppets it offers and to purchase the ones selected. Behind the web server, the company maintains a database that keeps all the product information including pictures, the stock of each of the products and pricing information. It also maintains information about customers that are currently or have recently been involved in a purchase. So why would our company want to replicate the data?

The first reason is *fault-tolerance*. Our puppet company definitely wants to guarantee its customers 24/7 access to their system, despite failures. A failure can mean that the process running the database software fails, that the physical machine crashes, e.g., due to malfunctioning of the hardware, or that the connectivity between the client and the server system is (temporarily) interrupted, due to some network failure. To handle these failure cases, our company installs two copies of the database on different nodes. In such a case, where the entire database is replicated, a node is also often referred to as a replica. Now, if one of the replicas fails, then there is still one replica up and running. The system is able to tolerate the failure of one of the copies. This is also referred to as *high availability* as the service remains available despite failures. In most high-availability solutions, the replicas reside in the same local area network to allow fast communication between the two as depicted in Figure 1.1. A failure detection mechanism detects any failure, and the clients connected to the failed node are reconnected to the available node where request execution simply resumes. Such a solution, however, cannot handle network failures between clients and database as the client will not be able to reach any of the replicas. To address this problem, wide area replication can be used (see Figure 1.2). With wide area replication, the database replicas are geographically spread and each client connects to the closest replica. Even if a remote replica is not reachable, access to the local replica is usually provided. However, the latency of the wide area network introduces interesting challenges, and failover becomes more complex due to the possibility of network partitions.

A second major use for replication is *performance*, as it can help to increase *throughput* and reduce *response time*. Let us come back to our puppet store. As a first option, the company installs

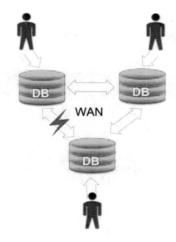

Figure 1.2: Wide area architecture

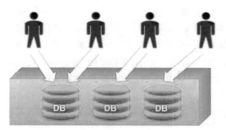

Figure 1.3: Cluster architecture

multiple replicas within a local area network, resulting in what is often called a cluster (see Figure 1.3). The cluster appears as one unit to the outside, and as requests come in, they are distributed across the replicas. By adding new replicas, the system can scale up to increasing demands. In this case, replication serves the purpose of *scalability* as it is able to provide increasing throughput.

However, as our company expands and attracts customers worldwide, it realizes that the quality of service for users that are far away from the company's headquarters suffers due to the long network delay for each message exchange. Therefore, the company also replicates its database at geographically strategic locations, providing acceptable response times to all their customers as they can now connect to a close-by replica. We call this *replication for fast local access*. At the same time, as more replicas are added across the world, the company is also able to increase the overall throughput of their system.

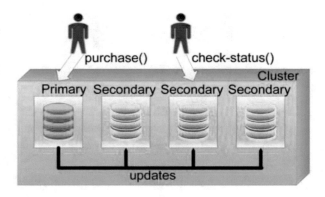

Figure 1.4: Primary copy approach

Cluster and wide area replication are not the only replication configurations. For example, assume the company also sells their puppets to toy stores and large department stores. Its saleswomen traverse the country, packed with their laptops to show the products to these stores and sell them in large scale. For that, they replicate at least parts of the database onto their laptops. This is a scenario where replicas are often in a disconnected mode, and the different replicas have quite different scale. Nevertheless, the purpose of replication remains the same: data remain available for the sales people although no network connection might exist, and the access is fast because it is local.

1.2   CHALLENGES

Despite its advantages, replication is not a straightforward technique to apply, and there are many hurdles to overcome before one has a suitable replication solution that fits the application requirements. We will discuss some of the issues in this book. At the forefront will be replica control: assuring that data copies remain consistent. Other issues are the architectural design options and autonomic support to provide self-management.

1.2.1   REPLICA CONTROL

When a data item is updated, its physical copies need to be updated. As easy as this might sound, this task, called replica control, is not a straightforward approach as there are many possible approaches, each having its advantages and its drawbacks depending on the application and the configuration. Let us illustrate this with an example. Assume our puppet company has decided to deploy a cluster of database replicas as depicted in Figure 1.4. Each node maintains a full copy of the database. When a client request arrives, it is redirected to one of the replicas that controls its execution. In most applications, there are two major request types: update requests, such as `purchase()` in the figure, update at least one data item; and read-only requests, such as `check-status()`, only read data items. Our company employs a *Read-one-write-all* (ROWA) replication strategy: the update of a data item is performed at all replicas, while a read operation accesses a single replica. ROWA can be implemented in various ways. The fundamental differences between existing approaches lie in where and when copies are updated [Gray et al., 1996]. In regard to *where*, our company uses a *primary copy approach*. There is one database replica that is considered the primary (replica). It holds the primary copy of the database. The other replicas hold secondary copies and are called secondary (replicas). All update requests are sent to the primary replica and are first executed there. An update request might read and write several data items. All writes are forwarded to the secondaries where they are also executed. Read-only requests can be executed at the primary or the secondaries. They can execute completely locally without coordination with other replicas.

In regard to *when* copies are updated, our company uses an *eager approach*, also referred to as *synchronous replication*. The secondaries apply the changes to their own copies immediately when they receive them, and then send a confirmation to the primary. Only when the primary knows that all secondaries have the changes, it confirms to the user that the execution was successful.

Primary copy vs. update anywhere.   The use of a primary replica forces all updates to be executed first at a single node. This simplifies the coordination of concurrent update requests. However, it has several disadvantages. For example, the primary can become a bottleneck. The alternative is to use an *update anywhere approach* (also called update everywhere). Each replica accepts both update and read-only requests and is responsible for their execution. While it avoids the pitfalls of the primary copy approach, it has its own problems. In particular, it is much harder to guarantee consistency as data copies might now be updated concurrently at different replicas.

Eager vs. lazy.   By using eager replication, the primary only returns a confirmation to the user once all secondaries have the updates executed. Thus, copies are "virtually" consistent. However, clients might experience prolonged response times due to the replication coordination. Especially with wide area replication, this can become a serious problem. Also network connectivity can be spotty in wide area networks, and the entire service might render unavailable if one replica is not reachable due to network problems. The alternative is to use *lazy replication*, also called *asynchronous replication*. With lazy replication, an update request is completely executed at one replica, which propagates the writes to the other replicas after returning a confirmation to the client. Thus, the coordination tasks do not affect the user. However, maintaining consistency is more difficult, as the same update takes place at different times at the various replicas.

Additionally, when lazy replication is combined with update anywhere, two updates concurrently submitted to two replicas can update the same data item and succeed. Later, when the updates are propagated, the system has to detect such conflict, possibly undo one of the updates despite the fact that the client was already informed that the update was successful.

Transactions.   Although we have not yet mentioned it, but to many readers, it will probably already be obvious that many of the applications that require replication will also require transactions and their properties – in particular atomicity, isolation and durability. In fact, it is pretty straightforward to map the execution of a client request to a transaction. Each request reads and/or writes several data items. From the outside, the execution of the request should appear as one logical execution unit. That is exactly the definition of a transaction. A *transaction* is a user-defined sequence of read and write operations on data items, and the system provides a set of properties for their execution. *Atomicity* guarantees that a transaction either executes entirely and commits, or it aborts not leaving any changes in the database. Thus, database systems provide rollback mechanisms to abort transactions and provide distributed commit protocols for distributed transactions, i.e., for transactions that access data items residing on different nodes. *Isolation* provides a transaction with the impression that no other transaction is currently executing in the system. Concurrency control mechanisms such as locking are in charge of that. *Durability* guarantees that once the initiator of the transaction has received the confirmation of commit, the changes of the transaction are, indeed, reflected in the database (they can, of course, later be overwritten by other transactions). Sophisticated logging protocols guarantee durability despite individual node failures.

Replication does not make it easier to achieve these properties. In fact, replica control, atomic commit protocols and concurrency control often work tightly together to let a replicated system appear as a single transactional system. In this book, transactions will be first-class citizens in considering and analyzing replica control algorithms. Note that while the next chapter describes the transactional properties in more detail, we assume the reader to be familiar with transactions and the basic mechanisms to implement them. Appendix A provides a short introduction if this is not the case.

In total, Chapters 2, 3, 6, 7 and 8 are dedicated to replica control. Chapter 2 introduces consistency criteria, extending the traditional atomicity, consistency, isolation and durability properties of transactions to a replicated environment. Chapter 3 provides a first introduction to some basic replication protocols exploring in more detail the design choices eager vs. lazy, and primary copy vs. update anywhere. The following chapters then discuss individual replica control strategies in more detail. Chapter 6 is dedicated to eager replication. As snapshot isolation has become a very popular concurrency control mechanism in recent years, we dedicate the full Chapter 7 to it. Finally, Chapter 8 focuses on lazy replication.

1.2.2   OTHER ISSUES

Transforming an abstract replication solution into a concrete implementation is not a straightforward endeavor. There are many design choices when architecting a solution for a concrete environment. In Chapter 4, we present several important *architectural patterns*. One important issue is where the replication logic is implemented: within the database system or as an external middleware layer. The choice has strong influence on the replica control algorithms, performance, and maintainability. Another question is how write operations are actually executed at the replicas. Efficient handling is crucial as they have a major impact on the scalability of the system. *Partial replication* is another aspect. With partial replication, each data item might only be replicated on some of the nodes. The idea is to reduce update costs. An update has to be applied to all copies of a data item. The more copies exist, the higher is the update load in the system. Partial replication provides a tradeoff between providing enough copies to be able to distribute read requests and keep the update costs low.

Chapter 4 also introduces the main ideas behind using *group communication systems* to support database replication. Group communication systems provide powerful multicast and group membership protocols that turn out to be very useful to manage a replicated system and support replica control.

Chapter 5 discusses *performance*. We do not provide any performance comparisons of the many replication approaches that exist, as they often depend on specific configuration and engineering details. But as performance analysis plays such a crucial role in building the right solution, we do not want to completely ignore it. Therefore, we present a simple analytical model that provides insights into how far a replicated database system can actually scale. We only consider a few parameters, but they already indicate the level of variation among design choices, and how small optimizations can have a huge influence on the performance.

Chapter 9 presents the *self-properties* a replicated system should provide. A replicated system is never static. Nodes might fail, new nodes might be added to the system, and the load must be dynamically distributed across the nodes. Chapter 9 describes how a replicated system can manage these tasks in an autonomic way. It describes how a replicated system can be *self-healing* by automatically removing failed nodes from the system and recovering them after restart, *self-optimizing* by autonomously distributing varying load across replicas, and *self-provisioning* by determining dynamically how many nodes are required in order to handle the current workload. These self-properties are the fundamental building blocks for elastic computing, as it is now required for cloud computing.

Finally, Chapter 10 briefly outlines other topics related to database replication that are out of the scope of this book. For instance, databases are typically deployed as the backend-tier of multi-tier architectures, and data are often distributed across all tiers. Replication of any of the tiers should be coordinated with the other tiers. This chapter also shortly outlines other domains, such as data replication in mobile environments and peer-to-peer systems.

CHAPTER 2

1-Copy-Equivalence and Consistency

Replica control and the task of keeping data copies consistent is one of the main challenges when architecting a replication solution. In this chapter, we define what consistency means for replicated transactional systems.

2.1 REPLICATION MODEL

A database consists of a set of data items x, y, ... In a replicated database, there is a set of database nodes R^A, R^B, ... each of them having copies of data items. Thus, we refer to x, y, ... as *logical data items*, and each logical data item x has physical copies x^A, x^B, ... where R^A is the node (replica) on which x^A resides.

From the perspective of the application, a transaction is a sequence of read and write operations on the logical data items of the database. The transaction is ended with a commit or an abort request. The latter indicates that the updates executed so far need to be rolled back.

One of the tasks of replica control is to map the operations on the logical data items onto operations on the physical copies. The most common execution model is to translate a logical read operation $r_i(x)$ of transaction T_i to one physical read operation $r_i(x^A)$ on one particular copy x^A. And a logical write operation $w_i(x)$ is mapped to physical write operations $w_i(x^A)$, $w_i(x^B)$, ... on all copies of x. This is called a *read-one-write-all (ROWA) approach*. Thus, a transaction T_i can have sub-transactions on many nodes, namely on each node on which it accesses at least one physical copy.

For simplicity of the discussion, we assume in this and most of the other chapters full replication where each node in the system has a full copy of the database, i.e., copies of all data items. The terms "node" and "replica" are then used interchangeably. With full replication, an update transaction, i.e., a transaction that has at least one write operation, has sub-transactions on all nodes, while read-only transactions typically only access the copies of a single node, albeit it is possible to distribute the reads among several nodes.

ROWA works fine because in most applications reads by far outnumber writes. Hence, it makes sense to keep the overhead for read operations as small as possible. ROWA is not suitable when failures occur, as an update transaction cannot complete anymore once a single copy becomes unavailable. Therefore, a derivation is the *read-one-write-all-available*, or ROWAA, approach where write operations execute only on all copies that are currently available. We will see later what that exactly means.

Performing the mapping between logical and physical operations is not sufficient. Replica control must be tightly coupled with the mechanisms that achieve the transactional ACID properties: atomicity, consistency, isolation and durability. In fact, the ultimate goal is that the replicated system provides the same semantics as the original non-replicated system. This is what is termed as *1-copy-equivalence*: the replicated system behaves like a 1-copy non-replicated system [Bernstein et al., 1987]. The ACID properties are all related to providing well-defined consistency in the advent of concurrent access and failures. When replicating a database, due to the distributed execution and the possibility of node failures, if no extra measures are taken, one can easily end up with transaction executions that would be disallowed in a non-replicated system. This means that designing a database replication solution implies to take care of 1-copy equivalence. In this chapter, we look at each of the ACID properties individually and discuss what it means to provide this property in a replicated environment, i.e., what does it mean to extend it with 1-copy-equivalence.

Note that while we attempt to make this chapter self-contained, we refer to Appendix A for a detailed introduction to transaction management in a non-replicated system.

2.2   1-COPY-ISOLATION

Concurrent transactions need to be isolated from each other to maintain the consistency of the database. Current non-replicated systems provide a whole range of isolation levels, each of them achieving a different degree of consistency. These isolation levels have to be extended to understand the global execution in a replicated environment. Ideally, the execution in a replicated system provides the same level of isolation as the execution in a 1-copy-system system. Therefore, we refer to this property as *1-copy-isolation*. This book has a closer look at two isolation levels.

1-copy-serializability.   The most well-known and strongest isolation level in a non-replicated database is serializability [Bernstein et al., 1987]. Serializability requires the concurrent execution of a set of transactions to be equivalent to a serial execution of this set. The most common definition of equivalence refers to the ordering of conflicting transactions. Whenever two operations conflict, that is, they access the same data item, are from two different transactions, and at least one of them is a write operation, then their order should be the same in the concurrent and the serial execution. Figure 2.1 shows three executions, also called histories or schedules. Time is moving downwards. There are two transactions. T_1 reads data item x and y and writes z, and T_2 reads x and z, and writes y. In the first schedule S1, T_1 executes completely before T_2, and in the second schedule S2, T_2 executes completely before T_1. That is, both are serial schedules. The third execution, S3, is not serial (operations are interleaved) but serializable as it is equivalent to the second schedule. There are two conflicting pairs of operations ($r_1(y)/w_2(y)$ and ($r_1(z)/w_2(z)$)) and in both cases, T_2's operation executes before T_1's operation. Finally, the fourth execution is not serializable, as the first conflict is executed as in S1, and the second as in S2. Serializability can be easily shown by building the

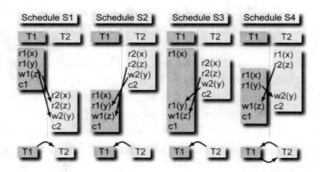

Figure 2.1: Serial, serializable and unserializable schedules

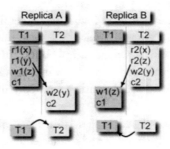

Figure 2.2: Locally serial, globally unserializable schedule

serialization graph of an execution where transactions are nodes and there is an edge from T_i to T_j if the two transactions have conflicting operations and T_i's operation is executed before T_j's operation. If the serialization graph is acyclic, the execution is serializable. Figure 2.1 shows the serialization graphs below the schedules, and we can see that S4 is unserializable because its graph has a cycle.

Moving to a replicated system, 1-copy-serializability extends this notion to the concurrent execution in a replicated system. Informally, 1-copy-serializability states that transaction execution in a replicated system should be equivalent to a serial execution of these transactions in a non-replicated or 1-copy-system. But what does this really mean? In a non-replicated system, there is only one copy on which all operations are executed while in a replicated system different operations execute on different copies.

A first attempt would simply indicate that as long as the executions at each replica are serializable, we are fine. Let us have a closer look at this. Figure 2.2 shows the execution of the same two transactions T_1 and T_2 at two replicas R^A and R^B. T_1 reads x and y at replica R^A and then writes z at both replicas. T_2 reads x and z at replica R^B and then writes y at both replicas. If you look only at the local execution at R^A, then this execution is serializable. In fact, it is serial with T_1 executing before T_2. Also the execution at R^B is serial, with T_2 executing before T_1. The problem is that this execution is obviously not serializable at the global level as the transactions conflict and they are executed in different order at the two replicas. There should be one common order. How can we formally express that something like this is not 1-copy-serializable?

Clearly, it is not enough that the execution at each replica is locally serial or serializable, but there must also be a relationship between them. The idea is to find a serial schedule over the logical data items, that is, a serial 1-copy-schedule, that orders all conflicting operations in the same way as all the local schedules in the replicated execution. Then, we can say that a replicated execution is 1-copy-serializable if there exists a serial 1-copy execution such that whenever one local schedule executes one of T_i's operations before a conflicting operation of T_j, then T_i is executed before T_j in the serial 1-copy execution. Looking at the example above, R^A requires the order $T_1 \rightarrow T_2$, and R^B requires $T_2 \rightarrow T_1$. Obviously, there is no 1-copy history that would be able to obey both of these orderings, and thus, 1-copy-serializability is not given.

Similar to serializability, we can check 1-copy-serializability with the help of serialization graphs. The serialization graphs in Figure 2.2 below the local executions at R^A and R^B are acyclic. In order to test for 1-copy-serializability, we can simply build the union of all the local serialization graphs of the executions at all replicas. Only if this union is acyclic, the global execution is 1-copy-serializable. In the example, the global serialization graph contains a cycle, and thus, the execution is not 1-copy-serializable.

Note that this rather informal description assumes that all replicas commit the same set of update transactions, and it does not consider node failures. Also, it is only valid if we assume full replication and a ROWA approach. A more formal definition can be found in Bernstein et al. [1987] and Kemme [2009].

In a non-replicated system, serializability can be achieved through a variety of concurrency control mechanisms, such as strict 2-phase locking or optimistic concurrency control. Given the example above, it is easy to see that it is not enough in a replicated system to let each node run its own concurrency control mechanism without coordination. Instead, local concurrency control needs to be extended to a replication concurrency control in order to achieve isolation at the global level. The next chapter presents several protocols based on strict 2-phase locking.

1-copy-snapshot-isolation.   There exist many isolation levels that provide less isolation than serializability. They allow more interleaving between transactions but some anomalies can occur [Berenson et al., 1995]. In this book, we only look at the very popular isolation level called *snapshot isolation*. It provides read operations a committed snapshot of the database as of transaction start, and only considers write/write conflicts. Commercial systems implement this isolation level by maintaining several versions for each data item. Avoiding conflicts between readers and writers has huge potential to increase concurrency. Snapshot isolation allows some non-serializable executions but avoids most of the well-known anomalies that can occur under lower levels of isolation.

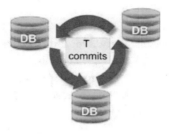

Figure 2.3: Coordination to achieve 1-copy-atomicity

In order to work in a replicated environment, snapshot isolation can be extended to 1-copy-snapshot-isolation in similar spirit as serializability. The execution in a replicated environment provides snapshot isolation if there exists a 1-copy execution that provides snapshot isolation such whenever one local schedule in the replicated execution performs two conflicting operations, the 1-copy-execution performs these two operations in the same order. We introduce snapshot isolation and 1-copy-snapshot-isolation in much more detail in Chapter 7.

2.3   1-COPY-ATOMICITY

Atomicity guarantees that a transaction executes in its entirety and commits, or it aborts and does not leave any effect in the database. That is, in case of abort any partial results have to be rolled back. A typical reason for transactions to fail is because of application semantics (e.g., balance of an account may not be below zero). Extending atomicity to 1-copy-atomicity in a replicated setting means that not only at a single replica all or none of the operations succeed, but that a transaction has to have the same decision of either all (commit) or nothing (abort) at all replicas at which it performs an operation. For the ROWA approach that we assume here, this means, all replicas in case of an update transaction, but only one replica in case of a read-only transaction. That is, all replicas should agree on the set of update transactions that are committed. Only then the 1-copy property is provided because a transaction that is committed at some replicas and aborted at others would be impossible in a 1-copy system. To achieve 1-copy-atomicity, some form of agreement protocol has to be executed among the replicas that forces all to make the same decision about the outcome of the transaction (Figure 2.3). Furthermore, if a transaction is aborted, its intermediate results need to be undone at all replicas. This second issue can be dealt with locally at each replica with the same mechanisms used in a non-replicated system.

A special atomicity case occurs when failures occur. In a non-replicated system, if a transaction was active (neither committed nor aborted) at the time of the failure, when the node restarts, it is no longer possible to commit the transaction. Thus, the system aborts it to make sure that it does not leave any partial changes in the system. We discuss the affect of active transactions in a replicated system further down.

2.4   1-COPY-DURABILITY

The durability property is related to atomicity. Durability guarantees that committed transactions are not lost even in the case of failures. When a node fails, it is typically restarted and the database recovered. In order to ensure durability, enough information has to be written to stable storage before the commit, e.g., via logging, such that at the time of recovery, the changes of committed transactions can be reconstructed.

Enforcing durability locally is not sufficient in a replicated system. When a node fails the other nodes usually continue execution, as a ROWAA approach requires only to write the available copies. When a node restarts and recovers, it does not only need to redo transactions that had been committed locally before the crash but also incorporate the changes of transactions that committed in the rest of the system during its downtime. This means a recovering node has to perform a global recovery in addition to the local recovery.

2.5   RELATIONSHIP BETWEEN ISOLATION, ATOMICITY AND DURABILITY

Isolation, atomicity and durability become highly related when we consider what happens in failure cases, in particular, when a replica fails when a transaction was in the middle of committing. In distributed database systems, such failures are a case for atomicity: atomic commit protocols such as 2-phase commit[1] among participants guarantee that all nodes decide on the same commit/abort outcome of a transaction despite failures. If one of the nodes fails before commit, all nodes need to abort the transaction as the failed node will abort the transaction upon performing local recovery. In cases where there is no replication, this is important because all updates on all data items need to be committed for the transaction to commit as a whole.

Replicated systems are conceptually different to a purely distributed database. In a replicated system using ROWAA, it is generally fine for a transaction to be still active on a replica that fails as long as it properly terminates at the available replicas. The failed replica's local recovery will undo the effects of all transactions that were active at the time of the crash and the global recovery procedure used for durability will transfer the changes of transactions that committed during the downtime.

Interestingly, atomic commit protocols also guarantee that a node cannot commit a transaction shortly before it fails but the others do not. Lazy protocols, as we have shortly mentioned in the introduction chapter, allow a transaction to commit locally at one replica and the updates are only propagated after commit. If the replica fails before the propagation, the other nodes will never receive the transaction. The transaction is lost. One can consider this "loss of durability" as the changes were not really durably entered into the available system. But we consider it a loss of atomicity. When the soon-to-be-failing replica commits the transaction, it was still available, thus, 1-copy-atomicity would require the other nodes to also commit the transaction.

---

[1] See Appendix A for a more detailed description of 2-phase-commit

Hence, what is needed for a ROWAA approach to behave correctly in regard to 1-copy-atomicity is that when a replica makes a commit/abort decision (whether it is available or fails shortly after making the decision), all replicas that are available and continue execution make the same decision.

A loss in 1-copy-atomicity also influences 1-copy-isolation and 1-copy-durability. As we discussed before, we can determine whether an execution is 1-copy-serializable by building the union of all local serialization graphs and check for cycles. Assume a failed node has committed a transaction while the other available nodes have not. It is not even clear how this transaction should be represented in the graph. Furthermore, when a failed replica recovers, one has to make sure that the results of these transactions are undone despite the fact that the transaction committed locally, as it did not commit in the rest of the system.

In the following chapters, when we discuss various replica control protocols, we analyze in detail the 1-copy-isolation and 1-copy-atomicity properties that each of them provides. We also distinguish whether protocols achieve 1-copy-isolation only in a failure-free environment, or also when failures can occur. 1-copy-durability is discussed specifically in Section 9.1, as its main task – bringing the state of the recovering replica up-to-date, is relatively independent of the replica control mechanism chosen.

2.6   1-COPY-CONSISTENCY

The only remaining ACID property that has not been discussed is consistency. Consistency is an overloaded term, used with different meanings in different contexts. In the traditional definition of the ACID properties, however, consistency refers to the requirement that a transaction, given a consistent database state, only performs changes that lead to another consistent database state. That is, the code of the transaction is correct from an application point of view and does not break the application-defined consistency of the database. The correctness of the transaction code is the responsibility of the transaction programmer. However, databases provide aids to monitor their correctness, e.g., by automatically checking pre-defined integrity constraints. The most common integrity constraints are primary keys that have to be unique and foreign keys that refer to records in other tables.

Not all replication protocols automatically guarantee 1-copy-equivalence if integrity constraints are defined over the database [Lin et al., 2009]. The problem is that databases, in order to guarantee integrity constraints, read additional data. As a formal discussion on integrity constraints can become quickly very complex, it will not be presented in this book.

2.7   SESSION CONSISTENCY.

Another consistency criterion that is somewhat related to 1-copy-isolation is *session consistency* [Daudjee and Salem, 2004]. Session consistency is the property that guarantees that a client observes its own updates. Clients often open sessions to the database system and submit several

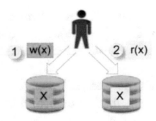

Figure 2.4: Violation of session consistency

transactions in a row. If one of the transactions updates a data item, then the next transaction should be able to read the change (unless, of course, a transaction in between has overwritten it). Session consistency is not captured by isolation levels such as serializability and snapshot isolation as they do not provide any guarantees for inter-transaction dependency. Nevertheless, non-replicated systems naturally provide session consistency as a committed change always becomes visible for transactions that start later.

   In a replicated system, however, this depends on how client connections are dealt with. If requests from a client are always executed by the same replica, then session consistency is again trivially enforced. However, as shown in Figure 2.4, when requests from the same client are processed by different replicas, it might happen that an update transaction T_1 is processed by replica R^A and then a later transaction T_2 is executed by replica R^B that still has not received or processed T_1's updates, Thus, T_2's reads do not see the values written by T_1 but a previous state. 1-copy session consistency is violated. In particular, this can happen with lazy replication as updates are only sent to other replicas after transaction commit.

2.8   EVENTUAL CONSISTENCY

Some protocols do not enforce any of the 1-copy-ACID properties because of the costs associated with achieving them. Thus, there exists a wide range of approaches that avoid these costs by relaxing the consistency model. In particular, we will see in the next chapter, that lazy update anywhere protocols belong into this category. Nevertheless, even those protocols attempt to provide a minimum of consistency [Malkhi and Terry, 2007; Saito and Shapiro, 2005; Vogels, 2008]. The best known minimalistic consistency criterion is *eventual consistency*. It guarantees that, should update processing cease for a sufficiently long time, the different copies of a data item eventually reach the same value. There are different techniques to attain eventual consistency.

   In its basic definition, eventual consistency does not care about transactions. Instead, it looks at each data item individually. Thus, it could happen that there are two transactions T_1 and T_2, both updating data items x and y, and at the end of execution and update propagation, x's last value reflects the update of T_1, and y's value reflects the update of T_2. 1-copy-serializability is clearly violated. There exist some approaches that aim at finding an eventual consistent solution that takes schedules into account [Kermarrec et al., 2001].

The promise of being consistent "some time in the future" is a far cry from 1-copy equivalence approaches and might be unsatisfactory for many applications. Therefore, consistency levels have been defined that *bound* the inconsistency that is possible. For example, the value of a copy may not differ from the true value or the values of other copies by a certain threshold, or a copy might not miss an update by more than a certain time. We will provide more details on these bounded consistency levels in Chapter 8 when we present algorithms that achieve them.

CHAPTER 3

Basic Protocols

In the introduction, we briefly discussed that replica control algorithms can be categorized by two parameters: where update transactions are coordinated and when updates are sent to other replicas. In principle, a protocol can be either eager or lazy, and follow a primary copy or update anywhere approach. From there, we can derive four basic categories: *eager primary copy*, *eager update anywhere*, *lazy primary copy* and *lazy update anywhere*. In this chapter, we give an example protocol for each of the categories, describe the general properties, and discuss the advantages and disadvantages of each of them in detail. Understanding the main implications of each of these categories is crucial in choosing the right replica control protocol for a given application and environment.

Replica control has to be coupled with the concurrency control and atomicity mechanisms of transaction management. For simplicity of illustration, our protocols are all based on strict 2-phase locking, also referred to as strict 2PL (we refer readers not familiar with strict 2PL to Appendix A for a short introduction), and ignore any form of failure. The protocol description also does not include unexpected aborts (e.g., due to the violation of an integrity constraint) or abort requests from the application.

We assume the same replication model as in Chapter 2. The database consists of logical data items x, y, ..., and has replicas R^A, R^B, ..., each having a full copy of the database. A transaction T_i performs a sequence of read operations $r_i(x)$ and write operations $w_i(y)$ on data items and then terminates with a commit request c_i. A transaction submits all its operations to one replica. This replica is called the *local replica* of the transaction, and the transaction is called local at this replica. We assume a ROWA approach where read operations are only executed at the local replica, and writes are executed at all replicas. Executing the writes at a remote replica creates a *remote* transaction. Thus, each logical update transaction has a local transaction at the local replica executing all reads and writes, and a remote transaction at each other replica containing only the write operations.

3.1 EAGER PROTOCOLS

3.1.1 PROTOCOL DESCRIPTION

In case of eager replication, our primary copy and update anywhere protocols are similar. The only difference is where update transactions can be local. In the case of update anywhere, any transaction can be submitted to any replica. In the case of primary copy, an update transaction has to submit all its operations to the primary replica. Read-only transactions, in contrast, can choose their local replica.

Upon: $r_i(x)$ for local transaction T_i
   1: acquire shared lock on x
   2: **return** x
Upon: $w_i(x)$ for local transaction T_i
     {for primary copy: only allow at primary replica}
   3: acquire exclusive lock on x
   4: write new value of x
   5: *send $w_i(x)$ to remote replicas*
   6: *wait until receive ok from all remote replicas*
   7: **return** ok
Upon: commit request for local transaction T_i
   8: **if** T_i *update transaction* **then**
   9:    *send commit(T_i) to all replicas*
  10: commit T_i
  11: release locks of T_i
  12: **return** committed
Upon: *receiving $w_j(x)$ of remote transaction T_j*
     {for primary copy: from primary replica}
  13: *acquire exclusive lock on x*
  14: *write new value of x*
  15: *send back ok*
Upon: *receiving commit(T_j) for remote transaction T_j*
     {for primary copy: from primary replica}
  16: *commit T_j*
  17: *release locks of T_j*

Figure 3.1: Eager protocols

Figure 3.1 depicts the basic structure of the combined replica and concurrency control protocols. The text in *italic* indicates the steps that are specifically needed for replica control. Other steps reflect the standard locking-based execution that is also needed in a non-replicated system. A transaction starts implicitly when it submits its first operation.

- Read operations are handled as in a non-replicated system (lines 1-2). They acquire a shared lock, and then return the current value of the data item.

- A write operation also performs first the standard steps (lines 3-4), acquiring an exclusive lock and writing the new value of the data item. Then, the write operation is sent to the remote replicas because a write operation has to be performed at all replicas (line 5). Only when the local replica has the ok's from all remote replicas (line 6), it informs the client about the successful execution (line 7).

Figure 3.2: Eager primary copy execution example

- At the remote replicas, the remote transaction is handled similar to local transactions. When a write operation arrives, an exclusive lock is requested, and the write operation executed (lines 13-14). Then, the local replica is informed about the successful execution (line 15).
- When the transaction submits the commit request, if it is an update transaction, first all remote replicas are asked to commit (lines 8-9 and 16-17), and only then the transaction is committed locally, the locks released and the confirmation returned to the client (lines 10-12).

3.1.2   EXAMPLE EXECUTION

Figure 3.2 shows the example of an execution under the eager primary copy protocol with two transactions. Transaction T_1 first reads x and then writes it. Transaction T_2 is a read-only transaction reading x and y. R^A is the primary replica and R^B a secondary replica. Time passes from top to bottom. Client requests and their responses are shown as arrows going to/from a replica. Communication between replicas is shown as arrows. Acquiring a shared/exclusive lock on data item x is denoted as $S(x)/X(x)$ and releasing a lock on x is denoted as $U(x)$ (U stands for unlock).

T_1 is submitted to R^A (it has to because it is an update transaction), and T_2 to R^B. Read operations are executed locally. After executing $w_1(x)$ locally, R^A forwards it to R^B. At R^B, T_2 currently holds a shared lock on x, thus, T_1 has to wait until T_2 commits and releases its locks. Then

T_1 can get the exclusive lock on x, execute, and return the ok to R^A. Only now the write operation completes. At commit time, R^A has to inform R^B and the transaction commits at both replicas.

3.1.3 EAGER PROPERTIES

Eager protocols are characterized by committing update transactions at all replicas in an atomic way. This provides strong properties.

- First, read operations never read stale data. Once they get a lock on a data item, it is guaranteed that this is the latest committed value in the system.

- Second, 1-copy-serializability is provided. As we have discussed in Chapter 2, 1-copy-serializability is violated if the union of the local serialization graphs has a cycle. For simplicity we only show here that a cycle of length two, i.e., a cycle of type $T_i \rightarrow T_j \rightarrow T_i$, is impossible. The reasoning for longer cycles is similar. The cycle is caused by two pairs of conflicting operations which we denote as $op1_i/op1_j$ and $op2_i/op2_j$. From each pair, at least one operation must be a write operation. Let us assume that one conflict is on data item x and occurs on replica R^A in the order $op1_i(x^A) < op1_j(x^A)$, and the other is on data item y and occurs on replica R^B in the order $op2_j(y^B) < op2_i(y^B)$. This means that T_i acquires the lock on x^A and T_j on y^B. In order for T_j to execute $op1_j(x^A)$, T_i must release the lock on x^A. Using strict 2PL it will only do so after having acquired the lock on y^B. But T_j will only release its lock on y^B once it has the lock on x^A. Therefore, this execution is not possible under strict 2PL [1].

- A third property is that 1-copy-atomicity is easily provided if there are no failures because at commit time all update operations have successfully executed at all replicas. Therefore, the commit will succeed at all replicas.

- In order to handle failures, some extensions are necessary. First, if a replica fails, a failure detection mechanism needs to inform all surviving nodes. Second, active transactions that were local on the failed replica have to be terminated properly. We have to consider two cases.
  In case (i), the client has not yet submitted the commit request. An example is shown as timepoint $tp1$ in Figure 3.2. The surviving replica R^B does not know whether it has received all write operations of T_1 so far. If there is more than one surviving replica, it is also not guaranteed that all have received the same set of write operations. Therefore, aborting the transaction is the easiest to achieve 1-copy-atomicity. In case (ii), the client has already submitted the commit request. This is shown as timepoint $tp2$ in Figure 3.2. The problem with the protocol described so far is that it is possible that the local replica has sent the commit request to some of the remote replicas but it crashes before all receive it. Or it commits the transaction without anybody having received the commit request. In this case, 1-copy-atomicity would be violated as some would commit, others abort the transaction. The use of an agreement protocol, such as the 2-phase commit protocol described in Appendix A, is necessary. This will guarantee that either all replicas commit the transaction or all abort it.

---

[1] In fact, it will result in a deadlock that will prevent the violation of 1-copy-serializability.

These strong properties, however, come with a price.

- First, a transaction can only commit when all replicas have executed the write operations. Thus, execution time is determined by the slowest node.

- Second, the 2-phase-commit protocol is expensive as it can block in case of failures, and it requires several sequential log writes to stable storage. We discuss in Chapters 6 and 7 some protocols that alleviate these problems, albeit still providing 1-copy-atomicity.

- Third, the combination of eager propagation and locking can delay execution considerably, as a long-running read-only transaction at any of the replicas can block an update transaction. Just assume in the example of Figure 3.2 that T_2 is a very long transaction. The more replicas there are in the system, the more likely it will be that there are conflicts between the readers and writers, limiting the possible scaleout. Thus, there have been many protocols proposed that avoid conflicts between update and read-only transactions executing on different replicas, or that eliminate locks and reduce the conflict rate between readers and writers, such as approaches based on snapshot isolation. We discuss them in Chapters 6 and 7.

3.1.4   PRIMARY COPY VS. UPDATE ANYWHERE

The obvious disadvantages of primary copy.   Looking at the base protocol in Figure 3.1, it is easy to see that primary copy is more restrictive than update anywhere as all update transactions have to be submitted to the primary replica. This leads to several disadvantages.

- First, we lose replication transparency. Clients need to know that the system is replicated and submit transactions according to their type to the primary or the secondaries. If the replicated system wants to transparently redirect update transactions to the primary and read-only transactions to the secondaries it must know at start of transaction its type. Several client interfaces, such as JDBC, provide a mechanism to declare a transaction read-only which can facilitate this. Update anywhere, in contrast, only requires the client to discover one of the replicas (we will see in Chapter 4 how to perform such replica discovery in a transparent manner to the client) and then submit all transactions, independent of their type, to this replica.

- A second disadvantage of primary copy is that the primary replica can become a bottleneck. Although the write operations are eventually executed at all replicas, the primary has to execute the read operations of all update transactions. If there are many update transactions, it might not be able to handle this load. Update anywhere is thus better suited for load distribution. Note, however, that in a read-intensive environment, this might not really be an issue.

- Finally, it is more difficult to achieve fault-tolerance with a primary copy approach. If the primary fails, another replica has to take over as primary requiring some fault-tolerant primary election mechanism.

The not-so obvious disadvantages of update anywhere.   So why would anybody use a primary copy approach? A major problem of eager update anywhere protocols that use locking is the possibility of a distributed deadlock. Let us have a look at the execution in Figure 3.3. T_1 and T_2 both write

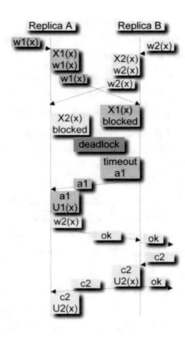

Figure 3.3: Distributed deadlock with eager update anywhere

x. T_1 is submitted to replica R^A and T_2 to R^B. Each transaction first gets the exclusive lock on x at its local replica and then forwards the operation to the remote replica where it is blocked. This scenario results in a deadlock, but none of the replicas can see this locally. As distributed deadlock detection is complex, it is likely that some timeout mechanism will eventually trigger the abort of one or both transactions. In the example, T_1 is the first to timeout, and R^B cannot return an ok to R^A but has to inform it about the abort. Then, T_2 can get the necessary locks, execute its operation and succeed. Handling all possible cases makes the protocol considerably more complex. Setting timeouts is tricky as a too short value causes many unnecessary aborts while a too high value blocks data items for a long time which can have a cascading affect and lead to deterioration. Gray et al. [1996] have argued that the likelihood of deadlock increases with a factor N^3 if N is the number of replicas in the system.

In contrast, it is simple to circumvent such deadlocks in the primary copy approach. The primary replica simply sends all write operations in FIFO order, and the remote replicas execute them in this order. The writes might only conflict with reads of local transactions. There might be deadlocks but they are always locally detectable at one replica. At the secondaries, there must be a read-only transaction involved in such deadlocks, which can then be the one to be aborted. Thus, the secondaries can guarantee that the writes will succeed.

In fact, a simplified variant of primary copy, called *primary/backup*, is frequently used for high-availability solutions. In this case, all transactions, whether update or read-only, are executed at the primary replica. The primary replica propagates all writes to the backups as in the primary copy approach. If the primary fails, one of the backups becomes the new primary. Clearly, in this case, replication is only used for fault-tolerance but not for scalability.

3.2   LAZY PROTOCOLS

3.2.1   PROTOCOL DESCRIPTION

Also in the case of lazy replication, the primary copy and update anywhere protocols are similar and depicted together in Figure 3.4.

- The read and write operations of transactions are first completely executed locally (lines 1-5). For the primary copy approach, update transactions can only be submitted to the primary replica.

- The commit is also executed locally and the locks released (lines 6-9). Only some time after the commit, all write operations are collected into a message and sent to all other replicas.

- Remote replicas, upon receiving these write operations, acquire all necessary locks (lines 11-12). In the primary copy approach, the writes are then executed (lines 13-15). Using update anywhere, things are more complicated. Update transactions can now execute concurrently at different replicas and update the same data items. Such conflicts need to be detected and resolved (lines 17-20). We will discuss this soon. Finally, the remote transaction is committed and the locks released (lines 21-22).

3.2.2   EXAMPLE EXECUTION

Figure 3.5 shows an example execution under the lazy primary copy protocol with two transactions. R^A is the primary replica and R^B a secondary replica. Transaction T_1 writes x and y. Transaction T_2 is a read-only transaction reading y. T_1 is submitted to R^A and T_2 to R^B. All operations are executed locally. After T_1 has executed all operations locally, it commits locally. Later R^A sends the set of all its write operations in FIFO order to R^B. At R^B, T_2 has already a shared lock on y when T_1's updates arrive. Thus, when T_1 requests exclusive locks on x and y it is blocked on y. When T_2 commits, T_1 has all the locks, finishes execution, and commits.

3.2.3   LAZY VS. EAGER PROPERTIES

The advantages of lazy propagation.   First, compared to eager approaches, lazy replication does not have any communication between the replicas while a transaction is executed. Only after commit are the write operations sent to the remote replicas. Thus, the response time for a transaction is not delayed by communication or coordination between the replicas. We can therefore expect lazy replication to have shorter response times than eager replication. The effect can be particularly big if replicas are distributed in a wide area network and communication latencies are large.

Upon: $r_i(x)$ for local transaction T_i
 1: acquire shared lock on x
 2: **return** x
Upon: $w_i(x)$ for local transaction T_i
      {for primary copy: only allow at primary replica}
 3: acquire exclusive lock on x
 4: write new value of x
 5: **return** ok
Upon: commit request for local transaction T_i
 6: commit T_i
 7: release locks of T_i
 8: **return** committed
Upon: some time has passed after an update transaction T_i committed
 9: *send collection of w_i of T_i in single message in FIFO order to remote replicas*
Upon: *receiving message from remote transaction T_j*
 10: *execute the following in receiving order*
 11: **for all** $w_j(x)$ *in message* **do**
 12:     *acquire exclusive lock on x*
 13: **for all** $w_j(x)$ *in message* **do**
 14:     **if** primary copy **then**
 15:         *write new value of x*
 16:     **else**
 17:         **if** Conflict detected **then**
 18:             *resolve conflict*
 19:         **else**
 20:             *write new value of x*
 21: *commit T_j*
 22: *release locks of T_j*

Figure 3.4: Lazy protocols

A second advantage is that a local transaction is not delayed by transactions running concurrently on other replicas. In Figure 3.5, the local transaction T_1 on primary R^A is not delayed by transaction T_2 executing at R^B. Only the remote transaction T_1 on R^B is affected, but this has no effect on the response time perceived by the user, who receives the confirmation when T_1 commits at R^A.

The disadvantages of lazy propagation.   A first problem is that 1-copy-atomicity cannot be achieved anymore if failures occur. If a replica executes and commits an update transaction and then fails, the other replicas will never get to know its existence although the user has received the commit

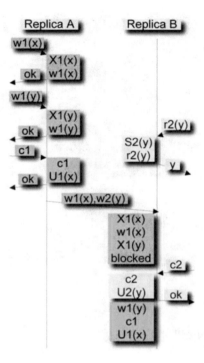

Figure 3.5: Lazy primary copy execution

confirmation. As already discussed in Section 2.5, this violates 1-copy-atomicity: the local replica has committed the transaction while it must be considered aborted at the available replicas. For instance, in Figure 3.5, if R^A fails after committing locally but before propagating the write operations, T_1 will never execute at R^B, and thus, there is no commit at R^B.

But even without failures lazy propagation provides inherently weaker consistency than eager propagation. For instance, at the moment a transaction commits at its local replica, the other replicas have stale data as their copies do not yet reflect the committed changes. Thus, read operations that read at the remote replicas before the write operations are propagated and executed, read outdated values. Lazy update anywhere is even worse than lazy primary copy. We discuss this in the next subsection.

3.2.4   PRIMARY COPY VS. UPDATE ANYWHERE

Some of the arguments that were presented in Section 3.1.4, when we discussed primary copy vs. update anywhere in eager approaches, also hold for lazy replication. Others get a new twist.

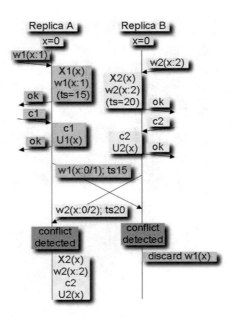

Figure 3.6: Conflicts with lazy update anywhere

The disadvantages of update anywhere.   We have already briefly mentioned the main problem of update anywhere and that is the level of consistency provided. Lazy primary copy can have stale reads, but 1-copy-serializability can still be achieved if there is a single primary replica that does not fail. Execution at the primary replica is serializable because it uses strict 2PL. The secondaries execute update transactions in the order they committed at the primary. Therefore, there is one global serialization order for update transactions. Read-only transactions are serialized locally at each secondary using strict 2PL.

Using update anywhere, however, transactions can now concurrently update the same data items on different replicas and commit without noticing the problem. Figure 3.6 shows an example execution with two transactions and two replicas. Both T_1 and T_2 write x. T_1 executes on R^A and T_2 on R^B. Both transactions first execute locally. After commit, both send their write operation on x to the other replica. If each replica blindly executed the write operation, R^A's copy of x would contain the value written by T_2, and R^B's copy the value written by T_1. The copies would have diverged. In order to circumvent such an inconsistency and achieve eventual consistency (both copies have the same value), replicas have to *detect* and *resolve* such conflicts.

Many systems detect conflicts by sending for each write operation the before- and the after-image of the updated data item. When a replica receives such an operation, it compares the current value of its own copy with the before-image. If they are different, a conflict exists. In the example of

Figure 3.6, assume that x has initially a value of 0, T_1's write sets it to 1 and T_2's write to 2. In this case, R^B detects a conflict when it receives T_1's write operation, as its own value for x is 2, while the before-image in T_1's message is 0.

Once a conflict is detected, it has to be *resolved*. The goal is that the different replicas agree on the same final value for their data copies. One among many possibilities is to use timestamps. Each replica timestamps its copy of a data item x with the local time when a write operation on x occurs, and these timestamps are piggybacked when the update is propagated. In the example of Figure 3.6, assume that T_1's write operations receives a smaller timestamp than T_2's write operation. In this case, when R^A receives T_2's write it first detects the conflict and then decides to apply the write operation as the timestamp is higher (20) than the local timestamp of x (15). In contrast, at R^B, T_1's write operation on x is not executed, as the timestamp is smaller than the local timestamp. At the end, both copies of x have the value written by T_2.

Conflict detection and resolution are complex, but they are not the only problem. Transactional properties are no longer guaranteed. In the example of Figure 3.6, T_1's client receives a commit confirmation, but its update was not committed at R^B due to the conflict resolution. 1-copy-atomicity is violated. Even partial results could remain. Conflict resolution is typically done on a per-object basis. Assume an extended example where T_1 and T_2 do not only update x but also y. Then, it could be possible that both replicas apply T_1's update on x and T_2's update on y. No non-replicated system that provides serializability could produce such a result.

The disadvantages of primary copy.   As with the eager protocols, lazy primary copy is less flexible than lazy update anywhere; it has a potential bottleneck, and fault-tolerance is more difficult to implement. What is worse, performance can now become a real deal-breaker. We just mentioned above that lazy replication does not require communication between replicas during transaction execution. This should translate in shorter transaction response times than with eager replication. But this is not necessarily the case in a primary copy approach when replicas are distributed in geographically distributed locations. Recall from Section 1.1, Figure 1.2, that this form of replication is mainly done to reduce the client-perceived response time. Clients connect to the closest replica avoiding long network delays between client and replica. However, in the primary copy approach, if a client wants to submit an update transaction, it has to connect to the primary replica, and that might actually not be close to the client. Thus, every operation the client submits traverses the long-distance link between client and primary. If a transaction has many read and write operations, it can easily lead to unacceptable response times. Lazy update anywhere does not have this problem, as each client can submit both read-only and update transactions to the closest replica.

3.2.5   SUMMARY

In this chapter, we presented four basic replica control protocols differing in where update transactions are executed and when write operations are propagated to other replicas. Each of the protocols has its advantages and disadvantages and none is a clear favorite. Instead, which protocol type to use will depend on many external factors, such as the replica configuration and the workload type.

Since this basic classification [Gray et al., 1996], a lot of work has been done in the area of replica control, and new protocols have been proposed in each of the basic categories *eager primary copy*, *eager update anywhere*, *lazy primary copy* and *lazy update anywhere*. Furthermore, some of the newer protocols can be considered hybrids that reside somewhere between the basic categories. Each of the new protocols aims in keeping the advantages of a certain category but eliminating, or at least alleviating its disadvantages. Some of the following chapters dig deeper into these new developments.

CHAPTER 4

Replication Architecture

This chapter is concerned with the architecture of replicated database systems. The protocols described in the last chapter were kept at a rather high-level without giving any details of how they could actually be implemented in a real system. This chapter introduces the basic design alternatives that exist for putting a replication solution into practice. The task of architecting a system consists of deciding what functionality is provided, how this functionality is packaged into subsystems, and how these subsystems interface. Understanding the trade-offs between various engineering alternatives is important as they have an influence on non-functional attributes such as availability, scalability, maintainability, etc.

The most crucial design decision one has to make is to decide where to locate the replication logic. The replication module could be an integral part of the database engine or it could be located in a middleware component that resides between the clients and the unchanged database kernel. For middleware based systems there exists again various architectural alternatives, such as whether there is a centralized middleware component, or the middleware itself is decentralized. The choice of architecture has a fundamental impact on how replica control is correlated with concurrency control, how clients connect to the system, how the replication module interacts with the database, and how update processing is performed. All these issues are dealt with in the first section of this chapter.

A second concern is how update transactions are actually processed at remote replicas. So far, we simply indicated that write operations are executed at all replicas. But once we consider that write operations are typical SQL statements, there are several practical issues to resolve. The second section is dedicated to update processing.

This chapter also discusses other important architectural issues such as replica transparency and replica discovery. The third section is devoted to this topic.

Finally, we discuss group communication systems as their use has become widespread in architecting database replication. The reason is that group communication systems help dealing with replica failure and recovery, as well as providing multicast primitives with ordering and reliability (atomicity) properties – which has proven to be helpful for enforcing 1-copy isolation, atomicity and durability. The fourth section provides an introduction to group communication systems and outlines how their functionality can be leveraged to architect database replication protocols.

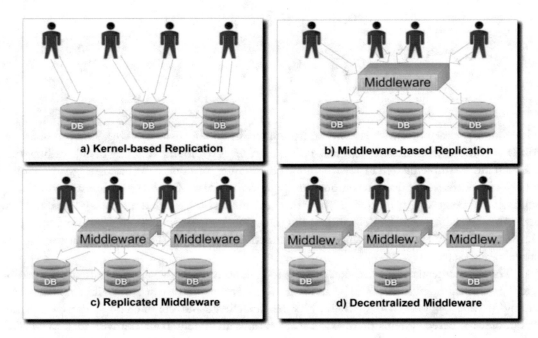

Figure 4.1: Alternative architecture

4.1   WHERE TO LOCATE THE REPLICATION LOGIC

4.1.1   KERNEL BASED ARCHITECTURE

The most natural location for the replication logic is the database kernel. Within the database kernel one has access to whatever functionality might be needed to replicate data and to integrate the replication logic with transactional processing. For example, it is quite easy to tightly couple replica control with the concurrency control mechanism. We refer to this approach as *kernel based* or *white-box database replication* since the database is like a white box with all its functionality visible to the replication module. This architecture is depicted in Figure 4.1.a. The database replicas coordinate with each other for replica control purposes. The clients typically connect only to one of the database replicas and only interact with this replica.

4.1.2   MIDDLEWARE BASED ARCHITECTURE

An alternative to kernel based replication is to encapsulate the replication logic into a separate component known as database replication middleware. The middleware is interposed between the database clients and the database replicas. Each database instance is a regular database without awareness of replication. From the database perspective, the middleware is simply a regular client.

The real clients send all their read, write, commit and abort requests to the middleware instead of the database. And the middleware is the one that takes care of coordinating transaction execution at the different database replicas, propagating updates, and ensuring that 1-copy equivalence is provided.

Centralized middleware.   A replication middleware in its simplest form can adopt a *centralized middleware* approach (see Figure 4.1.b). In this approach, there is a single instance of the middleware between clients and database replicas. It receives all client requests, schedules them, and forwards them to the relevant database replicas. It receives the replies from the database replicas and returns them to the corresponding clients.

Replicated centralized middleware.   The centralized middleware approach is simple, but unfortunately, it becomes a single point of failure. Thus, it fails to provide one of the main features replication is used for, namely availability. This problem can be avoided by replicating the middleware itself, purely for fault-tolerance purposes. Figure 4.1.c shows this architecture. One middleware is the master replica and all clients connect to this master, while the other is a backup middleware that only takes over if the master fails. We call this a *replicated centralized middleware*. As the middleware maintains some state (e.g., currently active transactions, some write information etc.), the backup middleware replica must receive state changes from the master middleware at appropriate synchronization points. There exist many different process replication techniques that are suitable to replicate the middleware such as active replication [Schneider, 1990]. However, in principle, the failover is similar to the failover of a database replica and we discuss this in more detail in Section 9.1.

Decentralized middleware.   A third alternative lies in having a middleware instance collocated with each database replica resulting in a *decentralized middleware* approach as depicted in Figure 4.1.d. The middleware replica and the database replica together build one replication unit. The middleware replicas communicate with each other for coordination purposes. Clients typically connect to one of the middleware replicas.

This architecture has two advantages over a replicated centralized middleware. First, there is typically only one failover mechanism for the unit consisting of middleware and database replica. In contrast, a replicated centralized middleware needs to implement different failover mechanisms for the middleware and the database replicas.

Second, a decentralized middleware is more attractive in a wide area setting. If there is only one (master) middleware, all clients have to connect to the same middleware which might be far from the client, even if one database replica is close. Thus, all interaction between client and middleware crosses the wide area link. Similarly, the single middleware might be close to some but not all of the database replicas, leading to long-delay communication between middleware and database replicas. In contrast, with a decentralized middleware, a client can connect to the closest middleware replica. Both the communication between client and middleware replica, and middleware replica and database replica is thus local and fast. Only the communication between middleware replicas is across the wide area network.

4.1.3   KERNEL VS. MIDDLEWARE BASED REPLICATION

Advantages of kernel based replication.   The major advantage of kernel based replication is that the replication module has full access to all the internals of the database system. Most importantly, it can be tightly coupled with the concurrency control mechanism. As shown in the algorithms of the previous chapter, concurrency control and replica control appear highly tangled, especially in eager approaches. In a kernel based approach that is quite easy to achieve. In contrast, a middleware approach does not have access to the concurrency control mechanism of the database system. Thus, many systems partially re-implement concurrency control at the middleware layer and might not be able to offer the degree of parallelism that is possible in kernel based systems. In particular, concurrency control in the database system is usually on a record basis, i.e., in locking based schemes, each record is individually locked just before it is accessed for the first time. In contrast, at the middleware we might not even know which records are accessed. Clients submit their requests typically in form of SQL statements and each individual statement can access many records. Thus, if the middleware does its own locking, it is typically on a coarse granularity such as tables. We also see shortly that executing write operations at remote replicas can be better optimized in a kernel based approach.

A second advantage of kernel based replication is that clients remain directly connected with the database system. In contrast, middleware systems introduce a level of indirection, leading to more messages in the system. However, middleware and database replica typically remain in the same local area network where this additional message overhead has relatively little impact.

Disadvantages of kernel based replication.   The blessing of kernel based replication, namely the large optimization potential, is also its curse. If replica control is too tightly interwoven with concurrency control or the processing of records, any change in their implementation will likely directly affect the replication module. Maintenance of the code becomes a problem. In contrast, middleware approaches are forced to separate the concerns as the replication module can only interact with the database through a well-defined interface. Thus, implementation changes within the database are unlikely to affect the middleware system.

An important hurdle for kernel based replication, many times unsolvable, is the requirement to access the source code of the database. In case of commercial database systems, only the vendor itself can implement the replication solution as no one else has access to the source code. For open source databases, such as PostgreSQL [PostgreSQL, 2007], there exist, in fact, several replication solutions. However, the internals of the database system are usually extremely complex, and modifying and extending the code needs considerable experience with the underlying system. In contrast, middleware systems are developed independently, possibly from third parties, and can decide on their own internal structure.

Finally, a kernel based solution is confined to a single database system. In contrast, a middleware system can possibly use different database systems, and thus, can implement a replication solution across a heterogeneous environment.

4.1.4   BLACK VS. GREY BOX MIDDLEWARE

One of the major disadvantages of a middleware approach is that it has a very restricted interface to the database replicas and it is difficult to take advantage of the functionality provided by the database. Systems that use only off-the-shelf database interfaces without any replication support from the database represent a *black-box replication* solution, as they see the database as a black box. However, in some cases, implementing some extra functionality within the kernel, and exposing or exporting this functionality through appropriate interfaces to the outside, can come a long way to help the middleware perform its replication tasks. We will see later several examples where such functionality is useful. In this case, we refer to a *gray-box* approach as the database replica is not completely replication oblivious.

4.2   PROCESSING OF WRITE OPERATIONS

Write operations have to be executed at all replicas, and processing updates is the main overhead of replication. Therefore, it should be done as efficient as possible. So far, we have simply indicated that the write operations of update transactions are executed at both the local and the remote replicas. In relational database systems, a write operation is typically an SQL update, insert or delete statement. Executing a write operation means parsing the statement, determining the number of tuples affected and then perform the modification/deletion/insertion. If all replicas indeed perform all of these tasks, then we call this *symmetric update processing*. However, this can quickly waste valuable resources. Second, it requires that execution of these operations is completely deterministic. An example of a non-deterministic operation is an update that sets an attribute to the current time. As operations do not execute at exactly the same time at different replicas, symmetric update processing would allow data copies to diverge.

   An alternative to symmetric update processing is what we call *asymmetric update processing*. When the transaction submits a write operation on data item x to a replica R^A, R^A does not immediately forward the write operation to the others even if the approach is eager. Instead, it first executes the operation locally, and then bundles the changes into a single message. That is, the identifier (e.g., the primary key) and the after-image of each updated record are collected. This information is sent to the other replicas, which can quickly find the affected records through their identifiers, and apply the updates directly. Applying these changes is much faster than executing the original SQL statement. In the following, we refer to the extracted changes as writeset, in order to indicate that this is different from the original write operations.

   Note that the concept of symmetric vs. asymmetric update processing is orthogonal to whether the replica control protocol is eager or lazy, primary copy or update anywhere, as most replica control protocols can use both of the update processing mechanisms.

   The question is how the writeset information can be extracted. Many different approaches have been proposed.

Triggers.   As a first option, the writeset can be obtained using triggers, a functionality widely available in most database systems. Whenever an insert/update/delete occurs, a trigger is fired that captures the particular changes. The trigger could write the necessary information into an extra table where it can be later retrieved. Triggers are heavily used both in kernel and middleware based approaches. Many systems have internal trigger mechanisms for various purposes that can be reused for writeset collection in kernel based replication. Most database systems also provide triggers at their interface, making them accessible to a middleware system.

Log mining.   Another possibility is to use the log mining facility available in some database systems. Databases usually write for each update performed the after-images of the affected records into a log. This is done for recovery purposes. Thus, writeset information can be easily extracted from the log. This appears particularly appealing for kernel based replication as they have direct access to the log. Some systems also export log access via interfaces. However, in this case, this is mostly, if not all, only after the transaction has committed. Therefore, middleware based approaches can only exploit this mechanism in case they use lazy replication where writesets are sent after commit.

Writeset extraction service.   Instead of awkwardly extracting writeset information through triggers or the log, the most efficient approach is to create them as the records are accessed. Just as logging creates before- and after-images while the updates take place, so could the writeset be built on the fly, being optimized for transfer over the network and application at the remote replicas. Clearly, such writeset creation can only be done in the database kernel. However, it would not be difficult to expose the functionality to the outside. And here comes the gray-box approach into play. Let us have a closer look at the options.

- *SQL writeset.* The writeset could be created as a list of simple SQL update, insert and delete statements where each statement writes exactly one record. Thus, instead of having complex SQL WHERE clauses, the reference is always only to the primary key. If the database allows the middleware to retrieve such a writeset, then applying the writeset at remote replicas simply means sending the individual SQL statements. Application should be faster than the original write operation as access to the records can always be through the primary key index.

- *Opaque binary writeset.* Another possibility is to obtain the writeset in binary form. This is more efficient, since it does not require transforming the internal record format into SQL. It requires, however, a complementary service to apply the binary writeset at remote replicas. This has also the additional advantage that applying the writeset avoids the overhead of SQL processing. The disadvantage is that the middleware cannot read the writeset. As we outlined before, middleware systems often re-implement part of the concurrency control. For that purpose, it might be helpful for the middleware to know exactly the records that were actually changed by an operation. Also, sometimes the middleware might want to do some additional processing, in which case it would also need the details of the changes.

- *Transparent binary writeset.* To avoid the disadvantages of the opaque binary writeset, the database could also provide an interface to access the content of the writeset. Thus, record identifiers could be extracted, which can be used, e.g., for conflict detection.

4.3   PARTIAL REPLICATION

The previous section discussed the possible performance gain of asymmetric update processing by avoiding to execute the full write operations everywhere. Nevertheless, although applying the changes might be faster, they still have to be applied at all copies. One way to further reduce the write overhead is to reduce the number of copies per data item. Using partial replication, each data item has only copies on some but not all of the nodes[1]. If a node does not host a copy of a data item then it does not need to apply the changes, leaving more capacity for doing other work. Therefore, the idea is to create just enough copies of a data item so that the read load on this data item can be nicely distributed among all copies.

However, partial replication has its own difficulties. In *pure partial replication* each node has only copies of a subset of the data items but no node contains a full copy of the database. In this case, it is possible that a transaction accesses a set of data items such that no node has copies of all of them. Thus, distributed transaction processing needs to be supported. This is complex as it requires exact knowledge of where data items reside. Also, the typical client interface for relational databases are SQL based, and SQL select statements can translate to read operations on many data items. All of these data items must reside on one node to perform the operation, but often it is not possible in advance to determine which set is actually going to be accessed. This reduces the flexibility of how the database can be distributed. For instance, it might require that all records of a table be collocated on a node.

Furthermore, update propagation is a further challenge. For instance, assume node N^A has copies of data items x and y, and node N^B has copies of y and z. Assume a transactions starts at N^A and reads x and then writes y. Later it submits a read (e.g., SQL select) operation that accesses y and z. This read operation can only be served by N^B, but this node might not yet have the current version of y, e.g., because the writeset is only propagated at the end of transaction. Thus, replica control becomes more complex.

There are two ways to avoid distributed queries. One is *hybrid partial replication*. In this approach, a set of nodes are full replicas that have a copy of the entire database, and another set of nodes are partial replicas containing only a fraction of the database. Hybrid partial replication analyzes each SQL statement and decides where to execute it. If there is a partial replica that contains all data items that might be accessed, then the statement can be executed at this partial replica. Otherwise, the statement must be executed at a full replica. The main issue with this approach is that full replicas have to apply all write operations. As the number of transactions increases, the full replicas will eventually saturate, building the bottleneck in the system. Figure 4.2 depicts pure and hybrid partial replication.

---

[1]In case of partial replication, we prefer to use the term "node" instead of "replica".

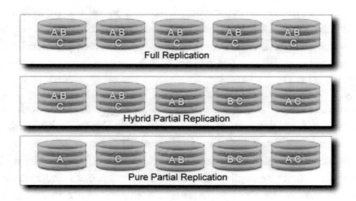

Figure 4.2: Full, hybrid, and pure partial replication

The other technique to avoid distributed transactions is to exploit a priori knowledge of transactions. If the set of transaction types and the data items each transaction might access are known in advance, then the database can be distributed such that for each transaction there is at least one partial replica that has all data items that will be accessed by the transaction. Therefore, each transaction can execute fully on one node.

In any case, deciding on where to put which data items in order to optimally exploit the resources of all nodes and to not create any bottlenecks in the system, is a challenging task and requires a good understanding of the application requirements. Furthermore, replica control can become more complicated in some cases. The replica control protocols we present in the following chapters all assume full replication although some might be easily extensible to partial replication.

4.4   OTHER ISSUES

Replication transparency.   A very desirable feature of any replication solution is replication transparency. It allows database applications to be kept unmodified. This is very important, since otherwise every database application would need to be modified to adjust for replication. That would make any replication solution hard to apply and maintain. From an architectural point of view replication transparency means that the replicated system has to provide exactly the same interface to the database application as a non-replicated database system. Databases are today accessed by means of database connectivity components such as JDBC and ODBC. These components are split into two modules, a client-side component and a server-side component. Clients connect to the client-side component that provides a standardized interface. Thus, whether middleware or kernel based replication is used, the application should be able to load a corresponding client-side component that offers the standard interface. The client-side component can now implement some of the replication functionality, hiding it from the application. In particular, two main functionalities that are usually implemented in the client-side connectivity component are replica discovery and failover.

Replica discovery.   In most of the architectures that we have discussed in Section 4.1, there is no longer a unique access point for clients. The only exception is the centralized middleware where there is a single middleware where all clients connect to. Otherwise, the middleware is replicated or decentralized, or the database replicas are directly accessed. Each of them has its own unique address, such as an IP address. Furthermore, this set is also dynamic, as replicas might fail and new replicas are added. This is in contrast to a non-replicated system where a client application connects to a well-specified single address. Therefore, the replicated system has to provide a mechanism to detect replicas. Let us have a look at two mechanisms to detect replicas.

- *IP-multicast-based replica discovery.* One possibility for replica discovery is to resort to IP-multicast. All replicas subscribe to a specific IP multicast address that is specifically used to detect replicas. When a client wants to connect to the replicated database the connectivity component at the client IP-multicasts a replica discovery message. Replicas receive the message and reply to it, typically with their real IP address, and possibly other information such as load and configuration information. The connectivity component can then select a replica to connect to according to the replies it received. In particular, in a primary approach it has to connect to the primary if it wants to submit update transactions. IP-multicast-based replica discovery is only possible if IP multicast is supported. Thus, it is typically restricted to cluster replication within a local area network.

- *Directory-based replica discovery.* An alternative is to rely on a directory service. In this case, a directory node with a well-known IP address keeps a directory of all available replicas and their IP addresses. The node monitors the current set of available replicas and updates the directory content regularly. Thus, the client connectivity component can request the directory information from the directory node and then connect to one of the available replicas. Of course, the directory node now becomes a single point of failure and might require replication by itself for fault-tolerance purposes.

Failover.   Failover functionality is somewhat related to replica discovery. When a replica fails, the clients that are connected to this replica have to reconnect to another replica. This is part of the failover procedure. Typically, when a node fails, the client loses the connection and receives a failure exception upon its next request. The client connectivity component has to transparently catch this failure, find a new replica and reconnect. To find a new replica, one of the discovery mechanisms above can be used. The client component could also have stored the available replicas when it made its first connection. Alternatively, information about available replicas can be forwarded regularly to clients by piggybacking it on standard messages transmitted to the client.

4.5   GROUP COMMUNICATION AS BUILDING BLOCK

A replicated database has to deal with many issues related to distribution: failure detection, coordination among replicas, reliable and ordered message exchange, etc. Providing such functionality is hard, especially in the advent of failures. But this challenge is not unique to replication, and a large body of research has proposed general-purpose solutions for these issues. In particular, group communication is a paradigm that provides most of these functionalities. This means that group communication is an excellent building block to simplify the architecture and protocols of a replicated database. In fact, over the last decade many replication solutions have been proposed that rely on the functionality of group communication systems to simplify the tasks at the replication layer. In the next sections, we give an overview of the key functionalities provided by group communication. Then, we shortly outline how replication can exploit these properties. More details will be given in the following chapters when we describe individual replication solutions in more detail.

4.5.1   GROUP COMMUNICATION AND RELIABLE MULTICAST

A group communication system is a communication middleware that provides an advanced interface to the application. It is typically implemented as a layer between the standard point-to-point communication (e.g., UDP/IP) and the application. Application processes are distributed over a set of nodes and communicate and interact via the group communication interface provided by the group communication layer. The group communication paradigm provides the notion of process group. The application processes build a process group that cooperates together for a given task, for instance, to replicate a database. The group communication layer provides two main functionalities: group membership and multicast. Furthermore, the two features are interrelated through the notion of virtual synchrony.

Membership.   Group membership provides the notion of views, where a view is the current list of connected and alive processes in the group. Application processes can join/leave the group by submitting a join/leave request. Furthermore, the group communication layer detects process failures and automatically removes the failed processes from the group. Every time that there is a change in the membership due to a join/leave or a failure, each available application process receives a *view change message* informing it about the membership of the new view.

Multicast.   Reliable multicast allows sending a message to all available group members. When multicasting a message one can specify reliability and ordering properties. This requires additional coordination within the group communication layer. Thus, when the group communication layer receives a message from the underlying network, it first ensures that the reliability and ordering properties are guaranteed. Only then the group communication layer *delivers* the message to the application layer.

Reliability.   In point-to-point communication, reliability means that a message will be eventually received by the receiver as long as both sender and receiver remain available. When a message is

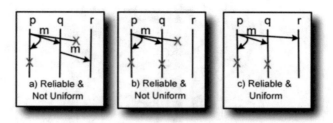

Figure 4.3: Reliable and uniform multicast examples

multicast to a group, we have many receivers. Thus, the concept of reliability becomes more complex. We can distinguish two levels of reliability, and their differences are subtle but important. They relate to faulty processes. For that, we have to first define what that means. We say that a process is *correct* if it is available, up and running, at least for the time period under observation. Otherwise, the process is *faulty*. Faulty means it crashes sometime during the execution of the message exchange. We only consider simple failures where a process simply stops working.

With this definition, *reliable* multicast guarantees that once a message is delivered to one correct process, it will be delivered to all correct processes. As a result, the same set of messages is delivered to all correct processes.

Let us have a short look at an example as depicted in Figure 4.3.a. There are three processes p, q and r building a group. While not depicted in the figure, each process has a group communication and an application layer. Assume the application layer of process p multicasts a message m to the group. Internally, the communication layer of p IP-multicasts m to the group or sends the message individually to the other processes using UDP. Since IP-multicast and UDP are unreliable, it might be possible that the group communication layer at p and q receive the message and deliver it to their application layers, but the message does not arrive at r. Now assume that p fails. We do not care whether the communication layer at p has delivered the message to its application, because reliable multicast does not care about faulty processes. However, since q is correct and the message was delivered, the message must also be delivered at r since r is also correct. Therefore, reliable multicast requires a resubmission mechanism so that the group communication layer at q can forward the message to r. This means that the group communication layers at correct processes have to keep track of the delivered messages and might need to forward them to other correct processes if failures occur.

An important aspect of reliable multicast is that it does not restrict what happens at faulty processes. Obviously, a message that is delivered by correct processes might not be delivered at a faulty process. But it might also be possible that a message is delivered at a faulty process while it is not delivered at the correct processes. Figure 4.3.b shows an example where p sends the message to

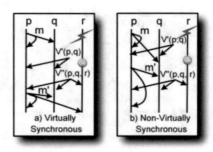

Figure 4.4: Virtual synchrony

q where it is delivered and then both p and q fail while the message never arrives at r and therefore, is not delivered at this correct process. This is allowed with reliable multicast.

Uniform reliable multicast.   Some applications also want to have control over what happens at faulty processes, and we will see later that this is true for database replication. Uniform reliable multicast provides stronger guarantees than reliable multicast. It guarantees that whenever a message is delivered at any process (independently of whether the process is correct or it is faulty and crashes shortly after delivery), then it is delivered at all correct processes. In this case, the execution of Figure 4.3.b is impossible, as a delivery at p or q implies a delivery at correct process r. It basically means that when the group communication layer of q receives the message from the network it does not immediately deliver it to the application. Instead, it waits until it knows that the communication layer of r has received it as well. Only then, it delivers the message. If it fails before receiving this confirmation from r, it is guaranteed that the message was not delivered to the application. That is, the fundamental property of uniform reliable multicast is that the faulty processes deliver a subset of the messages delivered at correct processes. Figures 4.3.a and b show cases that are prevented by uniformity. Figure 4.3.c shows the only case that would be allowed under uniformity in addition to no process delivering the message m.

Message ordering.   Group communication systems typically provide three levels of message ordering: FIFO, causal and total. With FIFO, ordering messages from the same sender are delivered in sending order to each group member. Causal ordering is the transitive extension of FIFO via casual dependencies. Total ordering guarantees that all messages are delivered in the same order to all group members independently of who sent them.

Virtual synchrony.   Virtual synchrony relates message delivery with view change events. Informally, it guarantees that each application perceives view changes at the same virtual time in regard to message delivery. More formally, virtual synchrony guarantees that two processes that transit from a view V to a consecutive view V' get the same set of messages delivered while being members of V. In the examples depicted in Figure 4.4, the current view V consists of p, q and r, and then r fails. Then, a view change message is delivered at p and q informing them that the new view V' consists of only p and q. In Figure 4.4.a a message m is delivered at p just before the view change V'. Under virtual synchrony, it is guaranteed that m is also delivered at q before the delivery of V'. Assume now that r rejoins. A new view change V'' is delivered at all three processes containing again the three processes. Under virtual synchrony, if a message m' is delivered at p after the delivery of V'' then m' is also delivered at q and r after delivery of V'' (unless they fail, of course). However, without virtual synchrony the scenario in Figure 4.4.b might happen. Message m is delivered at p but not at q before the delivery of V'. This violates virtual synchrony. The same happens with m' that is delivered at p before V'' and at q after V''.

4.5.2   SIMPLIFYING REPLICATION WITH GROUP COMMUNICATION

There exist many eager replication solutions that take advantage of some of the group communication primitives. We briefly outline how these primitives can be exploited to support replication semantics.

Exploiting group membership.   One of the functionalities required by replication protocols is membership. That is, a replication protocol should keep track of which replicas are available and connected. This functionality can be delegated to the group communication system by letting each replica be member of a replication group. In this way a failure of the node holding a replica is automatically detected by the group communication system. The replica could be a database replica in kernel based replication or a middleware replica if a replicated centralized or a decentralized middleware architecture is used. Basically, the group communication system detects the failure and produces a view change that is delivered to each available member of the group. This triggers the failover procedure at the replication layer. Group membership is not only useful for detecting failures. It is also useful to keep track of new replicas joining the system, either after a recovery of a failure or when new replicas join the system.

Exploiting ordered multicast.   Using an ordered multicast can simplify the task of replica control, and thus, helps to achieve 1-copy-serializablity or other 1-copy-isolation levels. Let us take as a simple example the eager update anywhere protocol of Figure 3.1 from Section 3.1. In Section 3.1.4, we outlined how this protocol can produce distributed deadlocks. The problem is that write operations can be submitted concurrently to different replicas, these replicas acquire the locks locally and then send the requests to the other replicas where they have to wait for each other. Such distributed deadlocks are difficult to detect. However, if a replica multicasts a write operation in total order, then the write operations are delivered to all replicas in the same total order. Now each replica only has to request locks in the order in which the write operations are delivered. As a result, all replicas acquire locks in the same global order, and distributed deadlocks can be avoided allowing only local deadlocks that are easier and cheaper to detect and resolve. We will see in later sections various protocols that exploit this total order to determine the global serialization order. In fact, the use of total order multicast often allows each replica to decide locally the serialization order of transactions, and whether a transaction can commit or has to abort because of conflicts.

Exploiting uniform reliable multicast.   Uniform reliable multicast can be used to guarantee 1-copy-atomicity despite failures. In Section 3.1 we have argued that eager protocols have to be enhanced with an agreement protocol, such as 2-phase-commit, to guarantee that all replicas decide on the same outcome of a transaction in failure cases. Instead, in the protocol of Figure 3.1, it is actually enough that the local replica multicasts the commit message to all replicas using uniform reliable multicast. If the message is delivered at any replica and the transaction committed, it is guaranteed that the message is delivered at all correct replicas, and thus, the transaction committed. In particular, once a message is delivered to the replica that sent it, and this local replica commits the transaction and informs the client about the commit, all correct replicas will commit, too. Therefore, even if the local replica fails shortly after the commit, it is guaranteed that the available system has the transaction committed.

Uniformity also simplifies recovery due to the guarantee that a failed replica has only committed a subset of the transactions that were committed by available replicas. Thus, recovery only has to send the missing transactions to the recovering replica, but there is no need to reconcile transactions that only committed at the failed replica.

One has to note, however, that implementing uniform reliable multicast requires by itself some agreement protocol. The group communication layer of a replica cannot simply deliver a message once it receives it but has to delay the delivery until it knows that the message has arrived at all other replicas. However, uniform reliable multicast is typically much faster than 2-phase commit because it is implemented in the communication layer, and more importantly, it does not use any logging to persistent storage (i.e., disk).

Exploiting virtual synchrony.   Virtual synchrony can come in handy at the time when a new node or a previously failed replica joins the system, and thus, can help with the task of 1-copy-durability. The joining replica needs the current state of the database. Typically, one of the available replicas transfers it. However, such a transfer can take a long time, and transaction processing typically continues during this transfer. The joining node may not miss the updates of any of these transactions, i.e., it either receives the updates of these transactions as part of the database transfer, or it has to execute these transactions by itself after the transfer is complete. Virtual synchrony can help to determine the point at which the joining replica switches to processing transactions by itself. For instance, the new replica could join the group shortly before the transfer is complete. A view change is delivered to all replicas indicating that the new replica has become member of the group. The replicas also know that all messages that are delivered after the view change are also delivered to the new replica. Therefore, the replica performing the transfer could transfer all changes related to messages delivered before the view change but let the new replica process all the messages that are delivered after the view change.

4.6   RELATED WORK

Basically, all of the early work on database replication and also the first approaches that appeared in the late 90s assume kernel based replication. Concurrency control at each replica is tightly coupled with replica control, providing one coherent replication solution. The replication solution is also tightly coupled with the other components of a database system. Most of these solutions are evaluated based on simulation, and thus, are not concerned with how these ideas can be truly implemented, either within a concrete database kernel or whether it would be actually possible to implement them in a middleware layer. Also, how write operations are actually executed at remote replicas is not clearly described in most of this early work.

A first concrete prototype implementation [Kemme and Alonso, 2000b] integrates an eager protocol based on group communication into the PostgreSQL engine. It directly extends the existing locking-based concurrency control mechanism and uses asymmetric update processing, taking advantage of the internal structure of records. A follow-up work [Wu and Kemme, 2005] moves the implementation to a newer version of PostgreSQL that is based on snapshot isolation. Manassiev et al. [2006] present a replication solution within the MySQL server. Little other research work on real kernel based implementations exists due to the complexity of database kernels and lack of publicly available database engines. In contrast, commercial systems all provide various forms of replication, typically embedded within the database kernel.

The seminal approach to middleware based database replication was Middle-R Jiménez-Peris et al. [2002b]; Patiño-Martínez et al. [2005]. Many middleware based approaches have followed [Amir and Tutu, 2002; Amza et al., 2003a,b; Cecchet et al., 2004; Elnikety et al., 2006; Lin et al., 2005; Röhm et al., 2002]. While most of the approaches use a black-box approach, Middle-R [Jiménez-Peris et al., 2002b; Patiño-Martínez et al., 2005] follows the gray-box approach as PosgreSQL is extended with two services to extract and apply opaque binary writesets. Another gray-box approach is Tashkent [Elnikety et al., 2006], which proposes to expose an interface to tag transactions with ordering that should be enforced by the database. In this way, writesets can be committed in parallel without the risk of the underlying database changing the ordering established by the middleware. Furthermore, Correia et al. [2007] and Salas et al. [2006] present reflective database architectures suitable to build gray-box replication. Reflection exposes database behavior to the middleware and, at the same time, permits the middleware to intercept the transaction processing within the database and add/change the behavior of the database. The C-JDBC [Cecchet et al., 2004] implementation has evolved into a commercial product.

Many black-box approaches use symmetric update processing, due to the difficulty of extracting the writeset. Exceptions are Ganymed [Plattner and Alonso, 2004; Plattner et al., 2006a] and DBFarm [Plattner et al., 2006b] that use triggers to extract writesets. The cost of writeset extraction and application has been analyzed in Salas et al. [2006].

Most middleware approaches are centralized. Basically, all decentralized approaches, whether kernel or middleware based, use group communication for communication among the replicas [Amir and Tutu, 2002; Kemme and Alonso, 2000b; Lin et al., 2005; Serrano et al., 2008;

Wu and Kemme, 2005]. Tashkent [Elnikety et al., 2006] uses a hybrid architecture in which local middleware instances are collocated with each database replica, and clients interact directly with these replicas. However, there is a centralized certifier with which all middleware replicas communicate for concurrency control purposes. This certifier is replicated for availability purposes. Another possibility for a hybrid approach would be to let clients connect to a centralized middleware that communicates with middleware instances collocated with each database replica.

Cecchet et al. [2008] discuss existing research attempts to middleware based replication and analyze what is needed to make them work in a real industrial setting. The main criteria are performance, availability and administration.

Most partial replication protocols offer 1-copy-serializability   [Fritzke Jr and Ingels, 2001; Holliday et al., 2002; Pacitti et al., 2005; Schiper et al., 2006; Sousa et al., 2001]. Fritzke Jr and Ingels [2001] use one total order multicast for every read operation and one for the writesets. Schiper et al. [2006] introduce partial replication algorithms based on group communication. In Holliday et al. [2002], one protocol requires all data to be accessed by a transaction to reside on one node, the other creates temporary copies for data items that are not locally replicated. Pacitti et al. [2005] describe a lazy replication protocol that allows both update anywhere and primary copy. For each table, a different mechanism can be used. It is a middleware based protocol that enforces the same total order of transactions at all replicas. There exists some work on partial replication and 1-copy-SI protocol [Serrano et al., 2007], its application to wide area networks [Serrano et al., 2008] and probabilistic analysis of abort rates Bernabé-Gisbert et al. [2008]. A performance analysis of partial replication was done by Nicola and Jarke [2000], and the question of where to locate replicas was discussed by Wolfson et al. [1997].

One of the first group communication systems to be developed was the ISIS system [Birman et al., 1991]. Further well-known systems are Totem [Moser et al., 1996], Horus [van Renesse et al., 1996], Ensemble [Hayden, 1998], Spread [Spread, 2007], Appia [Miranda et al., 2001], and JGroups [JGroups], with the last being frequently deployed in many open-source projects. A survey on group communication properties is provided by Chockler et al. [2001].

CHAPTER 5

The Scalability of Replication

One of the main objectives of replication is performance: providing scalability, increasing the throughput that is achievable by the system and/or reducing the response time of individual requests. All these metrics are influenced by many parameters, such as the specific replica control protocol, the underlying concurrency control, the chosen architecture, the message costs in terms of number of messages and message rounds, the network delay, the specific workload characteristics, and many more. The systems can have various bottlenecks that lead to saturation. The bottleneck could be the primary replica, the network and its delay, a large proportion of write operations, the concurrency control mechanism, the middleware, etc. Subtle differences in the configuration can have a huge impact on performance. Therefore, it is important that one is able to conduct effective performance experiments and to understand the performance results.

Performance analysis can be done by providing a real implementation and testing it using various benchmark applications, by developing a simulation study, or by designing an analytical model that depicts the influence of the main parameters. However, there do not exist many real implementations that compare a whole suite of solutions. The problem is that in order to compare all the different approaches in a fair manner, one would need to implement them all within a single framework, making sure that when comparing two solutions that differ in a specific aspect, all other parameters of the system remain the same. This is often unfeasible in practice.

Within the scope of this book it is impossible to provide a thorough analysis of all the issues that influence the performance of a replicated system. Therefore, in this chapter, we restrict ourselves to analyze a single performance metric, namely scalability, by using a simple analytical model that shows how three specific parameters influence this metric. In particular, we look at the percentage of write operations, whether symmetric or asymmetric update processing is used, and at partial replication. This analysis stands as an example of how a performance study can help understand the behavior of the system.

A system is scalable if the achievable throughput can be increased by adding more components to the system. In the case of a replicated database, this means that the transactional workload that can be handled by the system can be increased by adding more nodes to the system[1]. The more nodes, the higher should be the maximum throughput in transactions per time unit. Perfect scalability is given if an n-node system can achieve n times the throughput of a single node system, for arbitrary n. However, this is only possible if no coordination among the nodes is needed. If there are only read operations in the system, perfect scalability is possible as read operations can be easily distributed

---

[1]While in most of the book we prefer the term "replica" over the term "node" as we mostly assume full replication, use "node" throughout this chapter as we consider both full and partial replication, and we prefer to have a homogenous terminology.

across the nodes. However, updates have to be executed at all copies of a data item. As the workload increases, so does the absolute number of writes, requiring valuable resources on each node. These resources are then no longer available for read operations. But how much does this update overhead really influence scalability?

The analytical model that we present is very simple, and ignores many issues such as message overhead, concurrency control, the number of operations per transaction, the architecture, whether the protocol is eager or lazy, etc. Nevertheless, it provides a good first overview of the potential of scalability for a replicated system.

The metric that will be used for the scalability is the *scaleout*. It determines the number of times that a replicated system multiplies the maximum throughput of a non-replicated centralized system. For instance, a scaleout of 3 means that the replicated system achieves a maximum throughput that is 3 times the maximum throughput of a single node system.

5.1   MODEL

Our model assumes a ROWA approach where a read operation is executed at a single node and write operations are executed at all nodes with corresponding data copies, either through symmetric or asymmetric update processing. Furthermore, we assume an update anywhere approach where an update transaction can be executed at any node with the corresponding data copies.

We assume n to be the number of nodes in the replicated system, and w the fraction of write operations, i.e., $1 - w$ is the fraction of read operations. We also assume that all read and write operations have the same processing costs. Furthermore, assume C to be the capacity of a 1-node system in terms of operations per time unit it can process. In a non-replicated system C is exclusively used for executing local transactions, that is, productive work. However, in the replicated setup, a fraction of C at each node is devoted to installing writesets produced by other nodes. We term this remote work. Therefore, each node of the replicated system uses a fraction of its processing capacity for local work (L_i) and the remaining capacity for remote work (R_i), that is:

$$C = L_i + R_i \tag{5.1}$$

In a non-replicated system, the whole capacity is used for productive local work, i.e., $C = L$. The scaleout of the replicated system is the sum of the local (productive) work at each node divided by the productive work of a non-replicated system:.

$$scaleout = \frac{\sum_{i=1}^{n} L_i}{C} \tag{5.2}$$

That is, the scaleout indicates how many times the replicated system multiplies the capacity of a non-replicated system. The more local work a node performs, the better the scalability of the system.

Full replication and symmetric update processing.   In a fully replicated system with symmetric update processing each node has to perform as remote work all the write operations that are local at other nodes. This is:

$$R_i = w \cdot (n - 1) \cdot L_i \tag{5.3}$$

Given that $C = L_i + R_i$ we get:

$$C = L_i + w \cdot (n - 1) \cdot L_i \tag{5.4}$$

Solving the equation for local work L_i we get

$$L_i = \frac{C}{1 + w(n - 1)} \tag{5.5}$$

This means that the scaleout is:

$$scaleout = \frac{\sum_{i=1}^{n} L_i}{C} = \frac{n}{1 + w \cdot (n - 1)} \tag{5.6}$$

Full replication and asymmetric update processing.   When using asymmetric update processing, the remote load is lower because applying the writesets is cheaper than executing the write operations. Let the writing overhead, wo, be the fractional cost of applying a writeset with respect to fully executing the write operation. For instance, if applying the writeset takes 1/4 of fully executing the write operations, then wo would be 0.25.

In this case, the remote work for a node is $R_i = w \cdot wo \cdot (n - 1) \cdot L_i$, and therefore, $C = L_i + w \cdot wo \cdot (n - 1) \cdot L_i$. This results in $L_i = \frac{C}{1+w \cdot wo \cdot (n-1)}$. The scaleout for asymmetric update processing is then:

$$scaleout = \frac{n}{1 + w \cdot wo \cdot (n - 1)} \tag{5.7}$$

Partial replication and asymmetric update processing.   Finally, assume a data item has copies only at r nodes ($r \leq n$). Then, the remote work does not come from $n - 1$ but only $r - 1$ nodes. Thus, the remote work can be expressed as $R_i = w \cdot wo \cdot (r - 1) \cdot L_i$. This leads to the following scaleout[2]:

$$scaleout = \frac{n}{1 + w \cdot wo \cdot (r - 1)} \tag{5.8}$$

5.2   THE ANALYSIS

Our analytical model has only four parameters that influence the scaleout, namely the percentage of write operations, the number of nodes in the system, in case of asymmetric update processing the

---

[2]The calculation can also be argued in a different way. If the replicated system executes l operations submitted by clients then there are $l \cdot (1 - w)$ read operations executed at one copy and $l \cdot w$ write operations executed at all copies, one having the full cost, the others only having the asymmetric cost. Thus, the full capacity of the system is used as follows: $n \cdot C = (1 - w) \cdot l + w \cdot l \cdot (1 + (r - 1) \cdot wo)$ leading to $l = \frac{n \cdot C}{1+w \cdot wo \cdot (r-1)}$. The scaleout is the number of operations executed in the replicated system divided by the number of operations executed in a non-replicated system (which is C), resulting in the same scaleout formula as shown in Equation 5.8.

write overhead wo, and in case of partial replication, the number of copies per data item. Let us now have a look at how scalability is affected when we vary the values of these parameters. We first look at full replication, and then at partial replication.

Full replication and symmetric update processing.   Figure 5.1 shows the scaleout achievable (y-axis) with increasing number of nodes (x-axis) and different values of write percentage w (different graphs) for a system with full replication and symmetric update processing. With a workload consisting only of read-only transactions the scaleout is perfect. That is, a system with n nodes achieves n times the throughput of a non-replicated system. This is because no node needs to perform remote work and all capacity is available for productive local work. On the other extreme of the spectrum, with 100% write operations no scalability is attained ($scaleout = 1$) because every node is executing all write operations. An n-node system can handle the same load as a single node system. In between, we can see that the scaleout quickly worsens with increasing w-values. With 20% write operations, a 5-node system can produce 3 times the throughput of a 1-node system, while a 15-node system only increases this value to 4. With 50% writes, scaleout levels at 2. The higher the value of w, the earlier the time point that adding new nodes does not increase the overall capacity because most of the capacity of a node is used to process remote writes. The system saturates.

Full replication and asymmetric update processing.   Using asymmetric update processing, we have three parameters. In order to compare with symmetric processing, we fix wo to 0.3 and vary again the other two parameters. This value for wo has been taken from previous work that analyzed the writeset overhead in real systems [Jiménez-Peris et al., 2002b]. Thus, Figure 5.2 shows the scaleout again with increasing number of nodes and for varying values of w. Now, even with 100% write operations, some scalability can be attained (up to 3 for 15 nodes). For mixed workloads, the scaleout is even better. With 20% write operations, the scaleout with a small number of nodes is now very good, close to the optimal, and even with 15 nodes we can still achieve a scaleout of 8.

In summary, however, one can observe that scalability is limited in all cases. We can make writeset processing as efficient as possible, at some time point, as the absolute number of writes increases in the system, a node is mostly busy applying writesets and has little capacity left to do local work. As a result, as soon as the percentage of write operations is at a certain level, full replication will definitely not be able to scale to hundreds of nodes. Updates are an inherent limitation for the scalability of full data replication. Nevertheless, scaling up to 10s of nodes is already beneficial for many applications.

Partial replication and asymmetric update processing   Finally, let us have a look at partial replication. We fix $w = 0.2$ and $wo = 0.3$. Figure 5.3 shows the scaleout with an increasing number of nodes up to 15 nodes when there are 1, 2, 5, 10 and $n/2$ copies per data item. Scaleout is now very good. With only 2 copies, the scaleout is nearly optimal, and even with 10 copies a scaleout close to 10 can be reached for 15 nodes. It is interesting that, except for the case with $n/2$ copies, the scaleout does not seem to saturate. We analyze this in more detail in Figure 5.4, where we look at the scaleout up to 75 nodes. Indeed, we can see that the scaleout is linear in all cases except for $r = n/2$. The reason

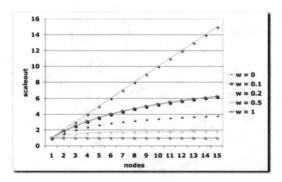

Figure 5.1: Scaleout of symmetric update processing with varying w

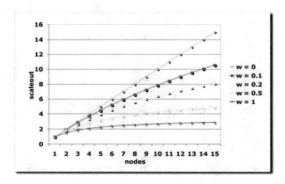

Figure 5.2: Scaleout of asymmetric update processing with varying w

is simple. The write load does not increase with the number of nodes because each data item has only a fixed number of copies, and therefore, the overhead to write a data item does not depend on n. In contrast, when the number of data copies increases with the number of nodes, as in $r = n/2$, then saturation will be reached. Thus, if it is possible to partition data in such a way that transactions only access one partition and the workload is equally partitioned across all partitions, linear scaleout can be achieved if the number of copies per data item remains constant.

5.3 RELATED WORK

As mentioned at the beginning of the chapter, comparing real implementations of various replication approaches is difficult because of the complexity of real implementations. Lin et al. [2007] provide a comparison of several replica control algorithms in a wide area setting in regard to response time and bandwidth consumption. Otherwise, nearly all studies are based on analytical models or simulations.

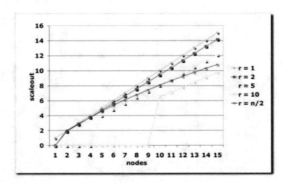

Figure 5.3: Scaleout of partial replication with varying number of copies

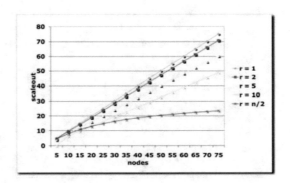

Figure 5.4: Scaleout of partial replication for large number of nodes

Simulation based comparisons have been performed, e.g., by [Carey and Livny, 1991], analyzing locking, timestamp and optimistic replica control mechanisms, and by [Wiesmann and Schiper, 2005] analyzing replica control mechanisms based on total order multicast.

Analytical studies have evaluated various aspects of replicated systems, for example, the impact of the location and number of data copies in partially replicated systems [Nicola and Jarke, 2000], the scalability potential of partial replication [Serrano et al., 2007], abort rates [Bernabé-Gisbert et al., 2008], quorum systems [Jiménez-Peris et al., 2003], and the performance of primary copy and update anywhere replication [Elnikety et al., 2009].

CHAPTER 6

Eager Replication and 1-Copy-Serializability

This chapter is devoted to eager replica control protocols providing 1-copy-serializability. As already mentioned several times, replica control is tightly coupled with concurrency control in order to achieve isolation at the global level. Database replicas are typically full-fledged database systems and already offer some form of concurrency control. In the case of kernel based replication, the existing concurrency control mechanism can be directly extended to work for the replicated environment. In case replica control is implemented on top of the database replicas in a middleware layer, this middleware typically has its own concurrency control mechanism. In some cases, it might be able to rely on the isolation mechanisms implemented within the database replicas to simplify the tasks at the middleware layer. In any case, it is possible that the middleware implements a different concurrency control mechanism than what is found within the database replicas.

This chapter only covers replica control protocols based on strict 2PL. 2PL, being pessimistic, avoids executions that might lead to a non-serializable schedule. Transactions have to wait for other transactions to terminate if they perform conflicting operations. There exist other well known mechanisms, such as optimistic concurrency control that provide serializability. It lets each transaction execute independently, and only at the end of transaction a validation takes place to see whether the transaction conflicts with other concurrent transactions. If this is the case, some transactions have to be aborted in order to guarantee that the execution remains serializable. Basically, no commercial database system uses optimistic concurrency control that provides serializability, and that might be one of the reasons why there exist few replica control protocols that are based on it. Nevertheless, the isolation level snapshot isolation can be implemented via optimistic techniques, and replica control based on snapshot isolation is very popular. The next chapter is devoted to replica control based on snapshot isolation and also briefly discusses an algorithm based on optimistic concurrency control that provides 1-copy-serializability.

Chapter 3 presented a pessimistic replica control protocol based on distributed 2PL. It followed a kernel based architecture as clients directly connect to the database replica. In this chapter, we focus on middleware based approaches. We present a suite of protocols that introduce, in a stepwise manner, the challenges associated with middleware based replication, and the issues that arise when using pessimistic concurrency control. The first protocol uses a centralized middleware and is a straightforward modification of the kernel based eager protocol presented in Chapter 3. The following two protocols discuss solutions with a decentralized middleware depicting the challenges and disadvantages that come with decentralization. They also show how asymmetric update processing can be deployed. For each of the protocols, we outline why 1-copy-serializability and 1-copy-atomicity is provided in the failure-free case, and we discuss whether 1-copy-atomicity is given in the failure case. The failover tasks that have to be performed so that clients can continue submitting requests to the system are discussed in detail in Section 9.1. Section 9.1 also discusses the recovery tasks needed to achieve 1-copy-durability.

6.1   CENTRALIZED MIDDLEWARE

We start with a centralized middleware approach. In this protocol, the centralized middleware performs replica control and concurrency control. It adopts a ROWA strategy with symmetric update processing where read-only operations are executed at any replica, and write operations are executed everywhere.

6.1.1   PROTOCOL

Figure 6.1 depicts the protocol. All clients are connected to the middleware and send their read, write and commit requests to the middleware. We ignore client induced abort requests for simplicity. The middleware performs concurrency control. For that purpose it implements a lock manager.

- When a client requests a read operation (lines 1-4), a shared lock is acquired and the operation is submitted to any replica as all replicas have the current state of all data items. When the replica returns the response, it is forwarded to the client.

- A write operation (lines 5-8) acquires an exclusive lock and is sent to all replicas. The middleware replies to the client once all replicas have executed the operation.

- At commit time (lines 9-11), the commit request is sent to all replicas that were involved in the transaction and the locks are released. For read-only transactions only a subset of replicas might be involved, for update transactions all replicas are involved.

- Since the middleware implements standard strict 2PL, deadlocks might occur (lines 12-15). But they are not distributed as the lock manager of the middleware has global knowledge of all locks. Thus, they are easy to detect and resolve at the middleware. One of the transactions involved in the deadlock needs to be aborted. The abort request is sent to all database replicas involved in the transaction; the locks are released and the abort information returned to the client.

6.1.2   EXAMPLE EXECUTION

Figure 6.2 shows an example execution of the protocol. In this example, there are two replicas R^A and R^B and two transactions. T_1 reads and writes x, T_2 is a read-only transaction that reads x and y. We show the execution at the middleware and its interaction with clients and database replicas but ignore the execution at the database replicas for simplicity. When T_1 submits its first operation, the middleware sets a shared lock on x and submits the operation to R^A. For the first operation of

Upon: $r_i(x)$ for transaction T_i
1: acquire shared lock on x
2: send $r_i(x)$ to any replica
3: wait until receive response from the replica
4: **return** x

Upon: $w_i(x)$ for transaction T_i
5: acquire exclusive lock on x
6: send $w_i(x)$ to all replicas
7: wait until receive ok from all replicas
8: **return** ok

Upon: commit T_i
9: send commit(T_i) to all participating replicas
10: release locks of T_i
11: **return** ok

Upon: deadlock
12: choose transaction T_i involved in deadlock
13: send abort(T_i) to all participating replicas
14: release locks of T_i
15: **return** aborted due to deadlock

Figure 6.1: Strict 2PL protocol with centralized middleware

T_2 it also successfully acquires a shared lock on x and the read operation is executed on R^B. When T_1's second operation requires an exclusive lock on x, it is not granted because it conflicts with T_2's shared lock, and T_1 has to wait. Then, T_2 needs a shared lock on y, which is immediately granted, and the read is performed, now on replica R^A. When T_2 submits the commit request, the middleware forwards it to all replicas and it releases all locks. The exclusive lock on x is now granted to T_1. The write operation is submitted to both R^A and R^B, as well as the commit later on.

6.1.3   ALGORITHM PROPERTIES

1-copy-isolation.   In principle, strict 2PL at the middleware provides 1-copy-serializability. The only difference to a non-replicated system is that the write operations are executed at all replicas, but as this occurs at the same time at all replicas, there is no conceptual difference. This reasoning assumes that the underlying database always reads the latest written version of a data item, i.e., if $w_i(x)$ was the last write operation on x before read operation $r_j(x)$, then $r_j(x)$ reads the value written by $w_i(x)$. This is typically given for database systems that implement locking themselves.

1-copy-atomicity in the failure free case.   In order to provide 1-copy-atomicity, database replicas must be able to commit/abort a transaction whenever the middleware requests it. Again, if the

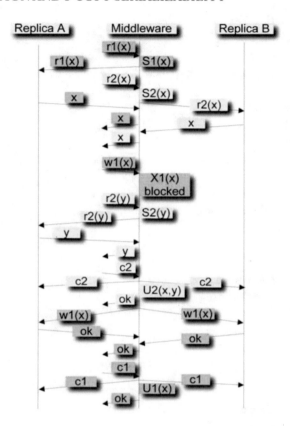

Figure 6.2: Example execution with centralized middleware

database system uses locking, this will typically be given. When a lock is granted at the middleware layer the lock will also be granted at the database replica and the operation will succeed. Thus, at commit time, the commit at each replica will be successful.

1-copy-atomicity in the failure case. We distinguish between failure of the middleware and failure of a database replica. If one of the database replicas fails, the middleware simply stops sending requests to this replica, following the ROWAA approach. The failure of the middleware is more complicated. Transactions for which no database replica received the commit request can be aborted by all database replicas. Transactions for which all database replicas received the commit are committed at all replicas. The problem is constituted by transactions for which some, but not all, replicas received the commit as 1-copy-atomicity is violated for these transactions. In order to guarantee 1-copy-atomicity for all transactions, the middleware and the database replicas must execute the commit using an agreement protocol such as 2-phase-commit.

Note however, that once the middleware fails, the system is no longer available, whether 1-copy-atomicity is provided or not.

Replicated centralized middleware. Using a replicated centralized middleware architecture, a backup middleware takes over if the master middleware fails. The backup middleware must receive enough information from the master middleware during normal processing in order to be able to take over in the case of failure, and to guarantee 1-copy-atomicity. Clients have to be reconnected to the new middleware. These issues are described in more detail in Section 9.1.

6.1.4 DISCUSSION

The protocol that we have presented in this section and the pessimistic protocol of Chapter 3 execute write operations synchronously at all replicas and require a 2-phase commit in order to guarantee 1-copy-atomicity in the failure case. With this, a transaction only commits if it is executed at all replicas. If one replica is highly loaded due to a complex read-only operation, all update transactions are delayed as their write operations at this replica will take a long time. The following two protocols avoid such behavior.

One fundamental problem of this and the following middleware based protocols is that client read and write operations are typically not explicit operations on individual data items. In relational database systems, the SQL interface uses declarative descriptions and a single statement can easily access many records of different tables. When concurrency control is implemented within the database kernel, the execution of a statement will eventually access the individual records, and this is the time point where locks are typically set. Therefore, the granularity of a lock is typically on a record level. However, the middleware only sees the original SQL statement and it is often impossible to know what records will actually be accessed. Therefore, a data item from the perspective of the middleware is much coarser, e.g., a database table, because they are easily extractable when parsing an SQL statement. As a result, concurrency is considerable restricted as transactions are more likely to conflict at the table level than at the record level.

6.2 DECENTRALIZED MIDDLEWARE

In this section, we discuss for the first time a replica control protocol that exploits group communication semantics in order to provide a fully decentralized solution.

Features. In Chapter 3, we have seen that independent execution of transactions on different replicas can lead to distributed deadlocks. Furthermore, both the protocol of Chapter 3 and the protocol of the last section lead to delays and blocking of update transactions if there are many concurrent read-only transactions in the system. Finally, they require an expensive 2-phase-commit protocol in order to guarantee 1-copy-atomicity in the failure case.

The protocol in this section eliminates these restrictions. Update transactions at each replica are executed independently, and as a result, a read-only transaction at one replica does not delay update transactions at other replicas. There are no distributed deadlocks. Furthermore, a 2-phase-commit is not necessary.

Main ideas.   The main idea to achieve these properties is to exploit the semantics of group communication systems to support concurrency control and failure handling. More specifically, by sending transaction requests in total order to all replicas, they are delivered at all replicas in the same total order. If they use this total order as guideline for the serialization order, transactions can be serialized in the same way at all replicas. Furthermore, by exploiting the delivery guarantees provided for multicast messages a message is delivered to either all or none of the replicas, guaranteeing 1-copy-atomicity in the failure case.

Restriction.   The presented protocol, however, has one major restriction, that is actually quite common for pessimistic middleware approaches. It expects that clients do not submit the individual read and write operations of a transaction but make a call that requests the execution of a transaction. Furthermore, given such a call, the middleware must be able to know what data items the transaction is going to access. Such setup is given in the following situations:

- Transactions are implemented as stored procedures within the database. A call to one of these procedures is a request to execute a transaction. The code of the stored procedures can be parsed in advance, and the SQL statements and the tables to be accessed can be extracted. Therefore, when a client makes a call to a stored procedure, the middleware knows all tables that are going to be accessed, and can perform concurrency control at the table level.

- Transactions are implemented as methods within application programs and an application server hosts the programs. The real clients make calls to these methods. Again the application programs can be parsed in advance, and the SQL statements and tables to be accessed by each transaction can be extracted. If the middleware is collocated with the application server, it can intercept the client requests, and knows the transaction and the tables to be accessed.

In both cases, it might even be possible to extract the data items to be accessed at a finer level. Stored procedures and program methods are typically parameterized and the client provides input parameters when it makes the call. Example parameters for a purchase transaction could be the client identifier and a product identifier. This might allow the middleware to determine the actual data records that will be accessed, and allow for concurrency control at a finer level. For simplicity, however, we assume in this chapter that all data items are tables.

Note that by knowing all statements of a transaction in advance, it is also easy to determine whether a transaction is an update or a read-only transaction.

6.2.1 PROTOCOL

The protocol is depicted in Figure 6.3. It uses not only symmetric update processing, it actually executes the full update transaction at all replicas. There is a middleware instance on top of each

Upon: submit of a read-only transaction T_i to R^j
1: request necessary shared locks for T_i in atomic step
2: wait until all locks are granted
3: execute T_i at the local database
4: release locks of T_i
5: **return** result
Upon: submit of an update transaction T_i to R^j
6: $T_i.replica = R^j$
7: multicast T_i in total order to all middleware replicas
Upon: delivering transaction T_i in total order at R^j
8: request necessary shared and exclusive locks for T_i in atomic step
9: wait until all locks are granted
10: execute T_i at the local database
11: release locks of T_i
12: **if** $T_i.replica = R^j$ **then**
13:      **return** ok

Figure 6.3: Strict 2PL protocol with decentralized middleware

database replica. For simplicity of description, we assume transactions are implemented as stored procedures within the database. However, the other option mentioned is conceptually similar. Clients connect to one middleware replica and submit their requests for transactions to that replica.

- When a client submits a read-only transaction (lines 1-5), the transaction is only executed at that replica. The middleware replica requests all locks in one atomic step, e.g., by putting the request operation into a critical section. When they are granted, the transaction is executed at the database. When execution completes (the transaction has committed at the local database replica), the corresponding locks are released, and the result is returned.

- When a client submits an update transaction (lines 6-7), the middleware replica firsts tags itself as the local replica, and then multicasts the transaction request to all replicas in total order. The total order multicast guarantees that even if different replicas multicast transactions concurrently, the requests are delivered to all replicas in the same order.

- When a transaction is delivered to a replica in the given total order (lines 8-13), all locks are requested, again within an atomic step, and when they are granted, the transaction is executed, and the locks released. Only the local replica returns the result back to the client.

6.2.2   EXAMPLE EXECUTION

Figure 6.4 shows an example execution. There are replicas R^A and R^B and transactions T_1 to T_3. We only show the actions at the middleware replicas MW^A and MW^B and their interactions with clients and the database replicas DB^A and DB^B but not the execution at the database replicas.

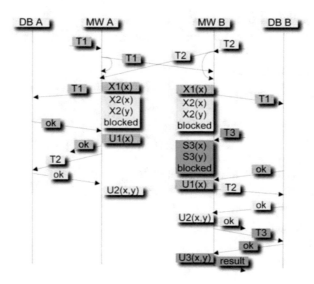

Figure 6.4: Example execution with decentralized middleware

There are two coarse-granularity items, x and y (e.g., tables). T_1 reads and writes x, T_2 updates x and y, and T_3 is a read-only transaction that reads x and y. T_1 is local at R^A and T_2 and T_3 are local at R^B. T_1 and T_2 are submitted concurrently to their respective replicas which multicast the requests in total order. T_1 is ordered first and T_2 second at both middleware replicas. Therefore, both acquire first the exclusive lock for T_1 on x and submit the transaction for execution to the local database. When T_2 is delivered at a middleware replica, it requests locks on x and y. The lock on y is immediately granted, but the lock on x must wait since there is a conflicting lock by T_1, and the transaction as a whole is blocked. Now, T_3 is submitted to MW^B, requests the locks on x and y and has to wait because of the exclusive locks by T_1 and T_2. When T_1 completes at a database replica, the corresponding middleware replica releases the lock on x, and the local middleware replica MW^A returns the confirmation to the client. Note that completion can occur at different times at the two replicas. Now T_2 gets its last lock, is executed and releases its locks on x and y. MW^B returns the ok to the client. Finally, T_3 gets all its locks at MW^B and executes completely locally.

6.2.3   ALGORITHM PROPERTIES

1-copy-isolation.   The protocol provides 1-copy-serializabiliy. Each local serialization graph is acyclic because each replica uses strict 2PL. Furthermore, the union of these local graphs cannot contain a cycle that consists of only update transactions. Conflicting update transactions are executed at each replica in exactly the same order as they acquire the locks in the same order due to the total order multicast. Therefore, if $T_i \rightarrow T_j$ in one local graph, then $T_i \rightarrow T_j$ in all local graphs.

Hence, if there is a cycle, it must contain at least two read-only transactions T_A and T_B that executed at replicas R^A and R^B respectively, and the cycle must be of form $T_A \rightarrow T_i \dots \rightarrow T_B \dots \rightarrow T_j \rightarrow T_A$, where T_i and T_j are update transactions. $T_i \neq T_j$ as otherwise R^A's serialization graph would have a cycle. $T_j \rightarrow T_A \rightarrow T_i$ means T_j acquired its locks before T_i on replica R^A. $T_i \dots \rightarrow T_B \dots \rightarrow T_j$ means that T_i acquired its locks before T_j on replica R^B. However, this is impossible as all transactions acquire locks in the same order at all replicas. Therefore, the union of all local serialization graphs cannot contain a cycle.

Of course, this reasoning assumes that the database replicas indeed perform all operations as requested by the middleware.

1-copy-atomicity in the failure-free case. The protocol has no deadlocks as all transactions acquire all their locks in an atomic step. Therefore, assuming deterministic execution of all transactions, there are no unilateral aborts, and all replicas commit the same set of update transactions in the failure free case.

1-copy-atomicity in the failure case. In order to handle the failure case, we have to analyze with which reliability level transactions are multicast. If we use reliable multicast it is possible that a replica multicasts a transaction; it is delivered locally; the replica executes it, commits it, returns the ok to the client and then fails before the transaction is delivered at any other replica. Thus, only the failed replica has committed the transaction while it has to be considered aborted in the rest of the system. Although this might be very unlikely, it is possible. Therefore, reliable multicast can lead to executions that violate 1-copy-atomicity.

If we use uniform reliable multicast, then we have the guarantee that whenever a message is delivered to any replica (even if the replica fails immediately after), the message is delivered to all available replicas. As a result, whenever one replica commits a transaction, all other available replicas also commit it. 1-copy-atomicity is provided.

6.2.4   DISCUSSION

As discussed before, compared to the protocol based on a centralized middleware, each replica executes the update transactions independently, and the local replica can return the ok to the user once the transaction has completed locally. It must not wait for the other replicas to execute the transaction. Therefore, any conflicts with read-only transactions on remote replicas have no impact on the response time seen by the client. Furthermore, no 2-phase-commit is necessary.

One major drawback of the presented protocol is the fact that all update transactions are fully executed at all replicas. First, this is even worse than symmetric update processing as even the read operations of update transactions are executed everywhere. Second, it requires transaction execution to be completely deterministic to guarantee that all transactions commit at all replicas. The next protocol we present eliminates these problems.

Upon: delivering transaction T_i in total order at R^j
1: request necessary shared and exclusive locks for T_i in atomic step
2: wait until all locks are granted
3: **if** $T_i.replica = R^j$ **then**
4:     execute T_i at the local database
5:     retrieve T_i's writeset WS_i
6:     multicast WS_i to all replicas (no order required)
7:     release locks of T_i
8:     **return** ok
Upon: delivering writeset WS_i of T_i at R^j
9: **if** $T_i.replica \neq R^j$ **then**
10:     apply WS_i at local database
11:     release locks of T_i

Figure 6.5: Strict 2PL protocol with decentralized middleware and asymmetric update processing

6.3   DECENTRALIZED MIDDLEWARE WITH ASYMMETRIC PROCESSING

This last protocol is a minor variation of the previous protocol. It implements asymmetric update processing, and hence, it allows for non-deterministic execution (see Chapter 4) and has better scalability (see Chapter 5).

6.3.1   PROTOCOL

The protocol differs from the previous protocol depicted in Figure 6.3 only in the actions that occur when a multicast update transaction is delivered in total order. Read-only transactions are handled exactly as in the previous protocol, requesting locks in an atomic step and executing completely locally. Similarly, update transactions are first multicast in total order to all replicas. Therefore, Figure 6.5 only shows the actions necessary when a transaction is delivered in total order. The replica requests the locks in an atomic step (lines 1-2) just as in the previous protocol. The differences start here. Only the local replica actually executes the transaction, and then multicasts the writeset to the other replicas before it releases the locks and returns to the client. No ordering is required (lines 3-8). The other replicas upon delivery of the writeset simply apply it before they release the locks (lines 9-11).

6.3.2   EXAMPLE EXECUTION

Figure 6.6 shows an example execution of the protocol. We use the same example as before with two replicas and three transactions. MW^A again multicasts T_1 and WS^B multicasts T_2, and T_1 is delivered before T_2 at both replicas. Both replicas set an exclusive lock on x for T_1 while T_2's lock on

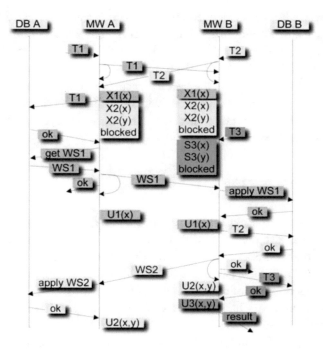

Figure 6.6: Example execution: decentralized middleware and asymmetric processing

x is blocked. But only MW^A submits the execution of T_1, extracts the writeset and multicasts it to all replicas. It then releases the locks and returns to the user. When its own writeset is later delivered, it simply ignores it. At MW^B, the writeset of T_1 is applied and the locks released. Now T_2 can get its lock, execute at R^B, the writeset is multicast and the locks released. When the writeset is delivered at MW^A, it applies it and releases the locks. MW^B submits T_3, once the locks of T_2 are released.

6.3.3   ALGORITHM PROPERTIES

1-copy-isolation.   The only aspect different to the previous algorithm is the asymmetry in processing the writesets. This has no effect on 1-copy-serializability.

1-copy-atomicity in the failure-free case.   Transactions do not need to behave deterministically to guarantee that all replicas commit the same set of update transactions.

1-copy-atomicity in the failure case.   We assume that the transactions are sent using uniform reliable multicast, but the writeset uses only reliable multicast. If a replica fails after having sent the transaction but before sending the writeset, the others have acquired the locks for this transaction but are blocked waiting for the writeset. They cannot simply abort the transaction and release the locks because the local replica could have already committed the transaction, but failed before sending the writeset.

There are two options to handle this case and avoid blocking. First, after being informed about the failure, all replicas could simply execute the transaction as in the previous protocol. Alternatively, one of the surviving replicas is assigned the task to execute the transaction and send the writeset to the others. In both cases, the transaction commits at the available replicas. The failed replica might have committed the transaction, or it was still active at the time of the failure. This is correct behavior and provides 1-copy-atomicity.

6.4   RELATED WORK

Eager replication has been explored extensively in the early 80s. Bernstein et al. [1987] summarize some of the work and also present a formal model of 1-copy-serializability. Several replication solution are proposed that combine replica control with a wide range of concurrency control mechanisms [Bernstein et al., 1987; Carey and Livny, 1991]. Failures, both node and communication failures, are a main focus of much of the work [Abbadi and Toueg, 1986; Bernstein and Goodman, 1984]. Some of these approaches have become well-known as they have appeared in several textbooks.

Since Gray et al. [1996] pointed out the limits of eager replication, a new wave of research started attempting to overcome those limitations. The idea of exploiting the ordering guarantees of multicast primitives is first explored by Agrawal et al. [1997]; Holliday et al. [1999]; Stanoi et al. [1998]. Kemme and Alonso [2000a] propose eager replication protocols based on total order multicast that provide different levels of isolation, among them 1-copy-serializability. All these solutions assume kernel based replication where the base mechanism is strict 2PL. Nevertheless, some of the approaches include optimistic extensions that detect conflicts between transactions executing on different replicas only at the end of transaction [Kemme and Alonso, 2000a; Pedone et al., 2003].

Postgres-R [Kemme and Alonso, 2000b] integrates a multicast-based protocol into a real database kernel (PostgreSQL). Building a serialization graph during transaction execution is another possibility to provide 1-copy-serializability [Anderson et al., 1998].

There exist many middleware based approaches that use pessimistic protocols [Amza et al., 2003a; Cecchet et al., 2004; Jiménez-Peris et al., 2002b; Kemme et al., 2003; Patiño-Martínez et al., 2005]. Kemme et al. [2003] propose a decentralized middleware where the database is partitioned, the full transaction is known in advance and transactions can only access a single partition. Concurrency control is based on data partitions and update transactions are fully executed at all replicas. The protocol in Section 6.2 is conceptually very similar. Jiménez-Peris et al. [2002b]; Patiño-Martínez et al. [2005] also use coarse granularity locking and require the data items to be accessed to be known in advance but transactions can access any arbitrary set of data items, and transactions use asymmetric update processing. The solution is based on a full-fledged replication middleware, Middle-R, on top of a relational database system. The protocol presented in Section 6.3

is similar to one of the protocols described in [Jiménez-Peris et al., 2002b; Patiño-Martínez et al., 2005].

Many protocols use a centralized middleware [Amza et al., 2003a,b; Cecchet et al., 2004] similar to what we describe in Section 6.1. Amza et al. [2003a,b] also require the data to be accessed and operation types (read/write) to be known at the start of the transaction so that locks can be requested at the transaction start time. The protocols described by Cecchet et al. [2004] allow read operations from different transactions to be executed concurrently at a given replica. However, at any given point in time only a single update, commit or abort operation is executing at a replica.

CHAPTER 7

1-Copy-Snapshot Isolation

So far, the book has focused on serializability and 1-copy-serializability as correctness criterion, implemented through locking. However, using locking, a single long lasting read-only transaction that scans entire tables can block many concurrent writers on these tables.

The mechanism simply does not scale to many concurrent transactions. Therefore, in practice, it is very common to increase concurrency by offering lower levels of isolation than serializability. Lower levels of isolation allow some non-serializable executions leading to what is referred to as anomalies but avoid some of the blocking or abort behavior. As long as the application can live with such anomalies, the throughput increase can be dramatic. In a replicated system that is designed for scaleout, it is even more important to offer high concurrency as a restrictive isolation level will easily become the bottleneck of the system leaving the available computational resources under-utilized. Scaling by adding new replicas will not help if concurrency control is the bottleneck.

In this chapter, we look at snapshot isolation (SI), which was briefly introduced in Chapter 2. SI is an isolation level very close to serializability, only allowing some very specific anomalies to occur. SI is implemented in many commercial database systems as it avoids read-write conflicts, i.e., read operations can always run fully concurrent to write operations without causing any conflicts. It turns out that concurrency control mechanisms that implement SI are very well suited for a replicated environment. As we have seen in the last chapter, re-implementing locking at the middleware layer leads to coarse-grained concurrency control, restricting the potential for concurrency. In contrast, it is fairly simple to implement middleware based replication based on SI.

In the following, we first introduce the concepts of snapshot isolation, and then present the notion of 1-copy-snapshot isolation (1-copy-SI) suitable for a replicated environment. We remain rather informal aiming in providing the reader a feeling of the fundamental principles behind this isolation level.

From there, we present a suite of replication protocols that provide SI. All protocols that we present are middleware based, showing that this isolation level can be achieved relatively easy outside the database kernel. All protocols rely on asymmetric update processing as this provides better scalability under update workloads. In all cases, we assume that the underlying database replicas provide SI. In fact, concurrency control is not completely implemented at the middleware layer (as was the case in the previous chapter), but it is distributed across middleware and underlying database systems. In particular, the handling of read operations is always left to the database replicas.

The first protocol that we present follows a primary-copy approach with a single middleware component. With this protocol the reader can get acquainted with the issues to be tackled by means of a relatively simple protocol. By resorting to a primary copy approach, handling of concurrent update transactions is concentrated on the primary, and the middleware has little to do in regard to concurrency control. The second protocol uses an update anywhere approach but still relies on a single middleware. As updates are now possible at all replicas, the middleware has to take over some of the concurrency control tasks. Finally, the third protocol adopts a decentralized middleware approach, exploiting group communication primitives similar to the decentralized protocols in the last chapter.

For each of the protocols, we outline why 1-copy-snapshot isolation and 1-copy-atomicity is provided in the failure-free case. 1-copy-atomicity in the failure case is also discussed. A detailed description of the failover procedure for each of the protocols is given in Section 9.1. Furthermore, 1-copy-durability is only discussed in Section 9.1.

7.1   1-COPY-SNAPSHOT ISOLATION

7.1.1   SNAPSHOT ISOLATION IN A NON-REPLICATED SYSTEM

Definition.   While snapshot isolation is an isolation level, it makes some assumptions about the implementation. In particular, it assumes a multi-version system. Whenever a transaction writes a data item x, it creates a new version of x. When the transaction commits, the version is *installed*. The order in which transactions commit determines an order on installed object versions. That is, if transaction T_i and T_j both write data item x, T_i commits before T_j, and no other transaction commits between T_i and T_j and writes x, then T_i's version is directly ordered before T_j's version of x.

Assuming such a multi-version system, snapshot isolation is defined through two properties: *Snapshot Read* and *Snapshot Write*. Snapshot read provides each transaction a snapshot of the database as of the time it starts: when a transaction T_i performs a read operation $r_i(x)$, it reads the version of x created by transaction T_j that was the last to write x and commit before T_i started. That is, T_i reads the version that was the last installed version at the start time of T_i. Writes that occur after the transaction starts are not visible. Snapshot write disallows two concurrent transactions (neither commits before the other starts) to update the same data item. This means that if two concurrent transactions attempt to update the same data item, one of them has to abort.

The snapshot read property provides high concurrency as read operations do not interfere with write operations. The snapshot write property helps avoiding some important anomalies as we will see shortly.

Examples.   Let us have a look at a few examples to get a better feeling for this isolation level. Figure 7.1 shows five schedules. As snapshot isolation is based on a multi-version system, we have to distinguish the various versions. We do so by tagging data item versions with the transaction that created it. For instance, a read $r_i(x_j)$ indicates that T_i reads the version of data item x that was created by transaction T_j, and a write $w_i(x_i)$ means that T_i writes x creating version x_i. We assume that an initial transaction T_0 has created initial versions of all data items.

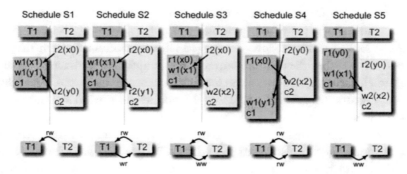

Figure 7.1: Example SI schedules

Schedule S1 shows an SI schedule where transaction T_1 writes x and y, while T_2 reads the two data items. The reading transaction T_2 reads from a committed snapshot, namely the versions written by T_0 and does not see the versions created by T_1. As a result, although T_2's read on y takes place after T_1's write, conceptually, it is ordered before the write because T_2 does not read the version written by T_1 but an earlier version. This makes the execution serializable. The serialization graph shown below the schedule has only an edge from T_2 to T_1.

In contrast, S2 is a schedule that is not allowed under SI. T_1 and T_2 have the same operations as in S1, but now T_2 reads the version of y written by T_1, which violates the snapshot read property. Note that this execution is not serializable as the serialization graph has a cycle.

S3 is also not an SI schedule. T_1 and T_2 are concurrent and both update data item x. This violates the snapshot write property. Note that S3 is also not serializable as shown by the cycle in the serialization graph. The schedule has the *lost update* anomaly. Both transactions first read x and then write it. Both read the initial version x_0. If the write operation is influenced by the preceding read operation, T_2 performs its write on the outdated value x_0. T_1's update can be considered lost. In general, SI disallows schedules with lost updates.

Schedule S4 shows a schedule that is possible under SI but is not serializable. As the transactions update different data items, the snapshot write property is not violated. However, T_1's read on x occurs before T_2's conflicting write, and T_2's read before T_1's conflicting write leading to a cycle in the serialization graph.

Finally, S5 shows a schedule that is actually serializable but not SI. As the transactions are concurrent and write blindly the same data item, the snapshot write property is violated.

Implementation.   Let us have a simplified view at how snapshot isolation could be implemented within a database system. We assume this implementation for our replication protocols. When a transaction T_i writes data item x, it creates a new version of x. During execution, this version is only visible to T_i itself (a transaction can see its own writes). Each version is tagged with the transaction identifier, which must be unique. When a transaction commits, it receives a commit timestamp from a commit counter that is increased upon each commit. When a transaction T_i performs a read operation $r_i(x)$, it looks for the version of x tagged with transaction T_j such that T_j committed before T_i started, and T_j has the largest commit timestamp of all transactions that wrote x and committed before T_i started. Therefore, when looking at transactions T_1 and T_2 in schedules S1 and S2 of Figure 7.1, execution would follow S1 and T_2 would read version x_0 because this is the last installed version when T_2 started.

Snapshot write requires that whenever a transaction T_i has updated a data item x and commits, and a concurrent transaction T_j also wants to update x, T_j has to abort. This can be implemented via locking or via a validation (or certification) phase at the end of transaction. Locking reflects a pessimistic implementation while using validation is an optimistic mechanism. We only look at the second alternative, simply because it is easier to describe. When the commit of transaction T_i is submitted, a validation takes place. It checks for each data item x written by T_i whether a concurrent transaction T_j that already committed also wrote x. If yes, T_i aborts by discarding its versions. If not, T_i's versions become the last installed versions. Certification has to be done in a critical session. This determines the commit order and also generates a total order on installed versions. When looking at Figure 7.1, validation of T_1 would succeed in all schedules as it is always the first to validate. For T_2, there would be no validation in S1 and S2, as T_2 is a read-only transaction. Validation would fail in S3 and S5 as T_2 writes the same data item x as concurrent transaction T_1, which already committed, and T_2 would abort instead of committing. However, in schedule S4, validation of T_2 would succeed as it writes a different data items than T_1.

Anomalies.   As just seen, SI allows some non-serializable schedules, thus, some SI executions have serialization graphs with cycles. However, the only cycles possible are those that include a double edge $T_1 \rightarrow T_2 \rightarrow T_3$, where both edges $T_i \rightarrow T_j$ are induced by T_i reading a data item x, and then T_j writing the next version of this data item [Adya, 1999; Fekete et al., 2005]. This can be observed in schedule S4 of Figure 7.1. Thus, in order to use serialization graphs for testing the SI property, the edges must be labelled with the type of conflict that caused the edge: T_i reads a data item and T_j creates the next version (rw), T_i writes a data item and T_j reads that version (wr), T_i and T_j write the same data item and T_j creates the version that follows T_i in the version order (ww). SI disallows all cycles except of those with consecutive rw-edges.

7.1.2   SNAPSHOT ISOLATION IN A REPLICATED SYSTEM

Moving to a replicated environment, it is, similar to serializability, not sufficient to guarantee that all local executions obey the SI rules. In fact, 1-copy-SI for a ROWA execution can be defined in the same spirit as 1-copy-serializability. A replicated execution is 1-copy-SI if

  i. The local execution at each replica follows the SI properties.

  ii. All replicas commit the same set of update transactions.

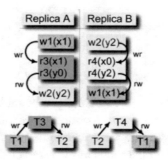

Figure 7.2: Execution that violates 1-copy-SI

iii. There exists a 1-copy execution that is allowed under SI such that whenever there is an edge $T_i \rightarrow T_j$ labelled with $rw/wr/ww$ in the local serialization graph of a replica, then the same edge occurs in the serialization graph of the 1-copy execution.

Similar to 1-copy-serializability, 1-copy-SI can be tested by looking for cycles in the serialization graph. In particular, one can test condition (iii) by building the union of the local serialization graphs. Condition (iii) holds if there are no cycles or only cycles that include two consecutive rw-edges.

In order to avoid any other cycles, it is crucial that each replica exposes the same sequence of snapshots to reading transactions. If this is not the case, 1-copy-SI is violated. Let us have a look at an example. In Figure 7.2, there are two replicas R^A and R^B. There are four transactions. T_1 writes x, T_2 writes y, and both T_3 and T_4 both read x and y. As ROWA is used, T_1's and T_2's writes execute at both replicas. Furthermore, T_3 executes at R^A and T_4 at R^B. At R^A, the execution is serial, executing first T_1, then T_3 then T_2. At R^B, the execution is also serial in the order T_2, T_4, T_1. Obviously, both local schedules are SI, and both replicas commit the same update transactions. However, the union of the serialization graphs contains a cycle $T_1 \xrightarrow{wr} T_3 \xrightarrow{rw} T_2 \xrightarrow{wr} T_4 \xrightarrow{rw} T_1$. This cycle does not contain consecutive rw-edges, and thus, the execution is not 1-copy-SI. The problem is that T_3 sees a snapshot where T_1 had committed but not T_2 while T_4 sees a snapshot where T_2 had committed but not T_1. Obviously, there is no 1-copy schedule that could fulfill both conditions.

7.2   PRIMARY COPY – CENTRALIZED MIDDLEWARE

This section presents a first protocol that provides 1-copy-SI in a replicated system. There is a centralized middleware that accepts all client requests and routes them to the proper replicas. When receiving the first operation of a transaction, the middleware must know whether it is a read-only transaction or an update transaction. In SQL implementations, typical client interfaces provide a mechanism to do such declaration, and we assume here that the middleware can distinguish between read-only and update transactions. Update transactions are executed concurrently at the primary but committed sequentially. The resulting writesets are propagated to the secondaries that apply them sequentially following the primary commit order. Read-only transactions are routed to any of the secondaries.

7.2.1   PROTOCOL

Figure 7.3 shows the protocol at the middleware. When the middleware receives the first operation, it decides on the replica that executes the transaction (lines 1-5). If it is an update transaction, it is the primary; if it is a read-only transaction, it is routed to one of the secondaries distributing the load among them. All following operations of the transaction are submitted to the same replica (lines 6-7). Update transactions are executed concurrently at the primary replica which provides SI executions. At commit time, read-only transactions are simply committed at their respective replica (lines 8-10). For update transactions (lines 12-18), the middleware extracts the writeset, commits the transaction, puts the writeset into the write queues that are maintained for each secondary, and returns the confirmation to the client. Commit might not be successful, as the SI mechanism in the primary might abort a transaction due to write/write conflicts with other transactions. In this case, the middleware informs the client about the abort. Writesets are applied and committed sequentially at each secondary (lines 19-20).

The middleware needs to be able to track the commit order at the primary in order to enforce the same order on the secondaries. This implies submitting commit requests sequentially to the primary and appending the writesets to the queues in this order. This can be achieved by putting these tasks into a critical section. If update transactions were not committed sequentially, inconsistent snapshots could become visible as discussed in Section 7.1.2. Note that different secondaries can apply the writesets at different speed.

In principle, an update transaction goes through three phases. In the *local phase*, the transaction executes at the primary. When the client submits the commit request, the *validation phase* starts. The middleware extracts the writeset and submits the commit at the primary which performs validation and terminates the transaction accordingly. If commit was successful, the *application phase* applies the writeset at the secondaries.

7.2.2   EXAMPLE EXECUTION

In all examples of this chapter, there are three update transactions T_1 to T_3. T_1 and T_3 write x, and T_2 writes y. There are two read-only transactions. T_4 first reads y and then x. T_5 reads x and then y. The transactions are depicted in Figure 7.4. The numbers before the individual operations indicate the order in which the clients submit these operations. Basically, the first operations of T_1 to T_4 are submitted, then the commit request of T_1, then the first operation of T_5 followed by the commit requests of T_2 and T_3. Finally, the remaining operations of T_4 and then the remaining operations of T_5 are submitted. We assume a transaction T_0 has created initial versions of x and y.

The execution is depicted in Figure 7.5. The middleware receives all operations from the clients. It sends the write operations of T_1 to T_3 to the primary, which executes them locally creating

Upon: receiving operation of transaction T_i from a client
 1: **if** this is the first operation of T_i **then**
 2:     **if** T_i is read-only **then**
 3:         assign a secondary to T_i
 4:     **else**
 5:         assign primary to T_i
 6: submit the operation to the assigned replica
 7: wait for response and return it to client
Upon: receiving commit request of transaction T_i
 8: **if** T_i is read-only **then**
 9:     commit at assigned secondary
 10:     return confirmation to client
 11: **else**
 12:     extract T_i's writeset WS_i from primary
 13:     commit T_i at primary
 14:     **if** ok returned **then**
 15:         append WS_i to writeset queues of all secondaries
 16:         return confirmation to client
 17:     **else**
 18:         return abort to client
Upon: WS_i is first in writeset queue of secondary S
 19: Apply WS_i at S and remove from queue
 20: commit at S

Figure 7.3: SI primary copy protocol

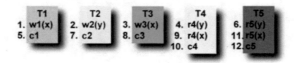

Figure 7.4: Transactions in example executions

new versions for each operation. The read requests of T_4 are sent to the secondary 1. The read operation on y returns version y_0, assuming that an initial transaction T_0 has created this version. T_1 is the first that wants to commit. The middleware first retrieves the writeset and then commits the transaction at the primary. The commit succeeds and the middleware applies the writeset at the secondaries. Now T_5 submits its first read operation, and the middleware forwards it to secondary

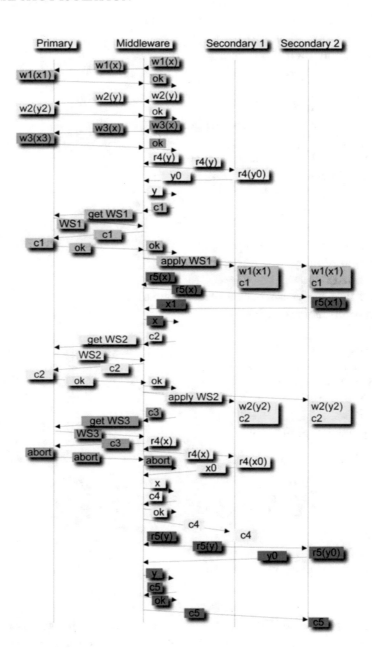

Figure 7.5: Example execution of SI primary copy

2. As T_1 has already committed at this secondary when T_5 starts, T_5 reads the version x_1 created by T_1. When T_2 submits the commit, the middleware retrieves the writeset, commits T_2 at the primary and applies the writesets at the secondaries. Although T_1 and T_2 are concurrent, they do not conflict, therefore T_2 commits. When T_3 submits the commit, the middleware retrieves the writeset, but the commit fails at the primary. The primary database determines that T_1 is concurrent to T_3 and conflicts; therefore, T_3 is aborted. The middleware, therefore, does not apply the writeset at the secondaries. The read operation $r_4(x)$ of T_4 executes at secondary 1. It does not read the update by T_1 but the original version x_0 as T_4 and T_1 are concurrent. Similarly, when the second operation of T_5 executes at secondary 2, it does not read the version created by T_2 as T_5 and T_2 are concurrent at secondary 2.

7.2.3   ALGORITHM PROPERTIES

1-copy-snapshot isolation.   1-copy-snapshot isolation is attained because of two mechanisms. First, all update transactions are executed at the primary that enforces SI locally. Second, update transactions are committed sequentially at the primary and writesets are applied sequentially in the same commit order at the secondaries.

Committing all update transactions in the same order at all replicas (primary and secondaries) is an important feature. In the example of Figure 7.5, T_1 and T_2 do not conflict; therefore, one might want to allow them to commit in different order at the secondaries, e.g., T_2 before T_1 at secondary 1, and T_1 before T_2 at secondary 2. Then, however, it could be possible that T_4 at secondary 1 reads the update of T_1 but not the update of T_2 while T_5 at secondary 2 reads, as in the current example, the update of T_1 but not the one of T_2. No 1-copy-schedule could observe both snapshots, and the union of the local serialization graphs would have a cycle that has no consecutive rw-edges. Therefore, this and all the following protocols ensure that transactions commit in the same order at all replicas.

With this, the three properties of 1-copy-SI are fulfilled. Property (i) is fulfilled because the underlying database replicas use SI. Property (ii) requires all replicas to commit the same update transactions. By executing the writesets of transactions that committed at the primary sequentially at the secondaries, there are no write/write conflicts at the secondaries, and thus, no aborts. Therefore, the secondaries commit the same transactions as the primary. The equivalent 1-copy schedule can be produced by using the local schedule of the primary for update transactions. This also reflects the sequence of snapshots that are produced at the secondaries. Therefore, any read-only transaction has seen one of these snapshots and can be ordered accordingly. In the example of Figure 7.5, T_4 reads a snapshot where only T_0 was committed, and T_5 reads a snapshot where T_1 was committed but not yet T_2.

1-copy-atomicity in the failure-free case.   1-copy-atomicity in the failure free case is automatically provided as 1-copy-SI already requires all replicas to commit the same set of update transactions.

1-copy-atomicity in the failure case.   We distinguish between failure of the middleware, failure of the primary, and failure of a secondary.

- If a secondary fails, the read-only transactions active on this secondary are considered aborted.

- If the primary fails, there are several transaction states to consider. (a) If the middleware has already received a commit confirmation from the primary, it also has the writeset, and thus, will apply it at all secondaries and the transaction commits at all replicas. (b) A transaction for which the middleware has not yet sent the commit request to the primary can be considered aborted. For both (a) and (b), the client should be informed about the respective outcome. If the middleware had sent a commit for a transaction T to the primary but the primary crashed before returning the confirmation, the primary might or might not have committed T. Although the middleware has already the writeset, it should not be applied at the secondaries, as the middleware cannot know whether validation succeeded or not. The transaction should be considered aborted and the client informed accordingly. This might violate 1-copy-atomicity if the primary committed the transaction. But this situation is acceptable as the client sees the abort, which is the decision within the available system, and the primary can roll back the changes at the time it recovers. However, 1-copy-durability becomes harder to enforce, since redo will not be sufficient to recover the primary, since such a transaction would need to be undone.

- If the middleware fails, 1-copy-atomicity is easily violated. As it applies writesets lazily, secondaries might have applied different subsets of writesets. It might even be the case that the primary committed a transaction and no secondary has the writeset applied.

Replicated centralized middleware.   In order to handle failure of the middleware, a middleware backup is needed. Sending writesets to the backup middleware and committing the transaction at the primary must be coordinated in an atomic fashion so that if the main middleware fails either the transaction committed and the backup has the writeset, or the transaction was not yet committed (and thus, will be aborted by the primary when it detects the middleware failure) and the backup does not have the writeset. The backup middleware must also have the means to determine whether for a given transaction, a secondary has already applied a writeset or not. Doing this properly can be quite tricky. We discuss a solution in Section 9.1.

7.3   UPDATE ANYWHERE – CENTRALIZED MIDDLEWARE

In this section, we present a protocol that avoids the bottleneck of a primary replica by resorting to update anywhere. Thus, all replicas share the update workload. However, it still uses a centralized middleware. Moving to update anywhere, the middleware needs to perform part of the concurrency control in order to isolate transactions that execute on different replicas. In particular, the validation of transactions is now performed by the middleware. As this is done at the end of the transaction and only requires access to the write operations, this is a fairly simple task, as the middleware has access to the writeset.

7.3.1   PROTOCOL

The protocol at the middleware is depicted in Figure 7.6. We can again distinguish several phases. The *local phase* executes a transaction locally at one of the replicas. In the *validation phase*, the middleware extracts the writeset and validates the transaction. If validation is successful, the *application phase* applies the writeset at the remote replicas. Each replica commits the transaction individually, once the writeset is applied locally.

The middleware keeps several variables. The variable *lastvalidated* is a counter of validated update transactions. The variable *lastcommitted[j]* keeps track of how many update transactions have already committed at replica R^j. Finally, *validatedSet* keeps track of previously validated transactions in order to perform validation. In the protocol description, this set is never garbage collected, but in a real implementation, transactions would be removed from this set as soon as there are no transactions that are concurrent to them.

The middleware assigns each transaction T_i a start timestamp $T_i.startTS$ and a commit timestamp $T_i.commitTS$. Whenever a transaction T_i is successfully validated at the end of execution, it receives the current value of *lastvalidated* as commit timestamp ($T_i.commmitTS :=$ *lastvalidated*). When a transaction T_i, starts at replica R^j, it receives as start timestamp *lastcommitted[j]*, that is, the commit timestamp of the last update transaction that committed at R^j ($T_i.startTS := lastcommitted[j]$). This helps the middleware to determine which transactions are concurrent. T_i is concurrent to T_j if $T_i.startTS < T_j.commitTS$ and $T_j.startTS < T_i.commitTS$.

Let us now have a look at the individual execution steps of a transaction.

Local phase. When the middleware receives the first operation of a transaction T_i, it selects a replica R^j at which T_i is local (lines 4-6). By submitting the operation to R^j, the corresponding transaction starts at R^j. It also assigns T_i a start timestamp that reflects the commit timestamp of the transaction that was the last to commit at R^j. Otherwise, read and write operation are simply executed by the assigned replica, and their results returned to the client (lines 7-8). This part of the protocol covers the local phase.

Validation phase. A commit request triggers the validation phase. If the transaction is read-only, it can simply commit (lines 9-11). Note that it is easy for the middleware to determine whether a transaction is read-only at the end of execution as it has seen all statements (e.g., only SQL select statements). If it is an update transaction, the writeset is extracted (line 13). The middleware performs the validation of the update transaction checking that there was no previously validated transaction T_j that was concurrent and had a write conflict (line 14). Note that T_j might not have committed at all replicas. What counts is that it was validated before T_i. If a transaction does not pass validation, it is simply aborted at the local replica (lines 15-16). If validation passes successfully, the transaction receives its commit timestamp. The transaction is added to the list of validated transactions and appended to the writeset queues of all replicas in FIFO order (lines 18-21).

Application phase. When a writeset is the first in the queue of a remote replica (lines 22-28), the writeset is applied and the transaction then committed. At the local replica, the transaction

Upon: Initialization
1: lastvalidated:= 0
2: lastcommitted[j]:= 0, for j=1...N
3: validatedSet:= ∅

Upon: receiving operation of transaction T_i from a client
4: **if** this is the first operation of T_i **then**
5:     T_i.replica:= select an available replica R^j
6:     T_i.startTS:=lastcommitted[j]
7: submit the operation to T_i.replica and wait for response
8: return to client

Upon: receiving commit request for T_i from a client
9: **if** T_i read-only **then**
10:     commit T_i at T_i.replica
11:     return confirmation to client
12: **else**
13:     Extract T_i's writeset $T_i.WS$ from T_i.replica
14:     **if** $\exists T_j \in validateSet: (T_i.startTS < T_j.commitTS) \wedge (T_i.WS \cap T_j.WS \neq \emptyset)$ **then**
15:         abort T_i at T_i.replica
16:         send abort notification to client
17:     **else**
18:         lastvalidated++
19:         T_i.commitTS:= lastvalidated
20:         append T_i to validateSet
21:         append T_i to writeset queue of each replica

Upon: T_i is first in writeset queue of replica R^j
22: **if** $T_i.replica \neq R_j$ **then**
23:     apply $T_i.WS$ at R^j
24: commit T_i at R^j
25: lastcommitted[j]++
26: remove T_i from writeset queue of R^j
27: **if** T_i.replica = R^j **then**
28:     return confirmation to client

Figure 7.6: SI update anywhere protocol with centralized middleware

can immediately commit as it was already completely executed. For each replica, the middleware keeps track of the number of committed transactions in order to synchronize with the start of new transactions.

Note that validation of writesets cannot be done concurrently in order to guarantee a global order of validation. Also, while a new transaction T_i is started at a replica R^j when the first operation is submitted (lines 4-6), no transaction should commit at this replica (lines 24-25) so that the middleware can be sure which transactions really committed before T_i started. Such behavior can be easily achieved by setting appropriate mutex locks.

7.3.2   EXAMPLE EXECUTION

The example uses the same five transactions as depicted in Figure 7.4. Figure 7.7 shows the execution. We omit the interaction between clients and middleware in order to simplify the figure. We assume two replicas R^A and R^B. T_1, T_2 and T_5 are executed at replica R^A, and T_3 and T_4 at R^B. We assume that a transaction T_0 created initial versions of all data items and received 0 as commit timestamp. Thus, $lastvalidated = 0$ initially. When receiving the first operation of T_1, the middleware assigns T_1 to R^A and sets the start timestamp to 0 (the commit timestamp of T_0) before submitting the write operation to R^A. T_2 and T_3 are assigned to R^B, and T_4 to R^A. All receive a start timestamp of 0, and their operations are submitted to the respective replicas. As all have the same start timestamp, it is clear that they are all concurrent. T_1 is the first to request the commit. The middleware receives the writeset and performs validation. As validation succeeds, T_1 receives 1 as commit timestamp. At R^A the transaction is simply committed. The middleware also keeps track of the fact that T_1 is committed at R^A ($lastcom[A] = 1$). At R^B the writeset is applied and T_1 committed. When the first operation of T_5 is submitted, the transaction is assigned to R^A. As R^A has already committed transaction T_1 with a commit timestamp of 1, T_5 receives this as a start timestamp, and it reads the version x_1 written by T_1. At commit of T_2, the middleware receives T_2's writeset from R^A, validates T_2 and assigns it a commit timestamp of 2. Validation succeeds because T_1 and T_2 do not conflict. However, the validation of T_3 fails. The middleware can detect that T_3 is concurrent to T_1 ($T_3.startTS < T_1.commitTS$), and they have a conflict. The middleware aborts T_3 at replica R^B. When T_4 performs its last read, R^B returns the original version x_0 as T_1 and as T_1 and T_4 are concurrent at R^A. T_4 can commit without validation. Similar, T_5 reads the original version y_0 of y as it is concurrent to T_2 at R^A, and it can commit without validation.

7.3.3   ALGORITHM PROPERTIES

1-copy-snapshot-isolation.   We only briefly discuss why all three properties of 1-copy-SI are provided. Obviously, all local schedules are SI as we assume the underlying databases use SI. Showing that all replicas commit the same transactions is not that obvious. We have to show that if the middleware decides to commit a transaction, the commit actually succeeds at all replicas. The clue is that the middleware keeps exact track of all concurrent transactions, and validation fails if there is any conflict with a concurrent, already validated transaction. Thus, once validation succeeds, the

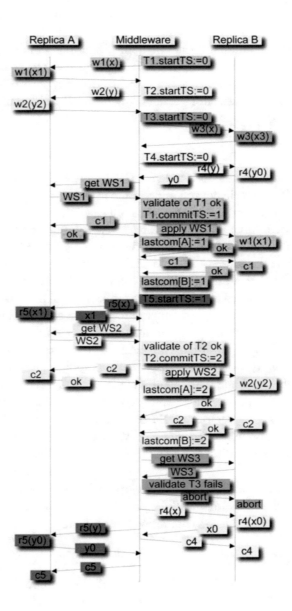

Figure 7.7: Example execution of SI update anywhere with centralized middleware

database will not find any further conflicts, and also commit the transaction. For property (iii), we use again the fact that all update transactions are committed in the same order at all replicas. Thus, this order can serve as guideline to build the 1-copy-schedule for the update transactions. Finally, as all replicas go through the same sequence of snapshots, read-only transactions can be ordered according to the snapshot they access.

In summary, use two main mechanisms to enforce the 1-copy-SI properties. First, we keep track of concurrent transactions and perform validation at a central point, the middleware. Second, writesets are applied and transactions committed in the order in which they are validated by the middleware.

1-copy-atomicity.   The arguments for 1-copy-atomicity are similar to Section 7.2.
- Atomicity in the failure free case is given because of 1-copy-SI.
- Failures of database replicas are simple to handle. If the transaction has already received the writeset of a transaction local to the failed replica, it will commit or abort in the remaining system according to the validation, and 1-copy-atomicity is provided. If the middleware has not yet retrieved the writeset, it can be considered aborted in the entire system, again guaranteeing 1-copy-atomicity.
- If the middleware fails, 1-copy-atomicity is easily violated. If a backup middleware is used, it has to receive writesets before they are applied at any replica, and also have appropriate information about the data structures maintained at the main middleware to continue validation. Furthermore, it must have the means to determine for each of the writesets it received, whether the corresponding transaction has already committed at a replica or the writeset has to still be applied. How this can be achieved is discussed in Section 9.1.

7.4   UPDATE-ANYWHERE – DECENTRALIZED MIDDLEWARE

In this section, we present a protocol that uses a decentralized middleware. In fact, the protocol of the previous section can be adjusted quite easily to follow a decentralized approach. We can take advantage of multicast primitives for the communication among replicas in order to support 1-copy-isolation and 1-copy-atomicity. Having a decentralized middleware avoids the complex failover of a replicated centralized middleware.

Each replica consists of a middleware and a database replica building a replication unit. Clients connect to any middleware replica. The middleware replica to which a client connects to becomes its local replica. The client interface remains the same. They can submit their read and write operations in the usual way.

The central middleware in the protocol of the previous section performed two roles, one was transaction validator, i.e., checking whether concurrent transactions had write/write conflicts, and the other was validation sequencer, i.e., determining the order in which transactions are validated. In the role of transaction validator, it kept track of the formerly validated transactions and their writesets and commit timestamps. Decentralizing this role means that each replica has to keep track of this information and perform validation.

In the role of sequencer, the central middleware has determined the validation order by entering a critical section. In a decentralized approach, coordination among the middleware replicas is needed to determine a total validation order. The idea is to use a total order multicast for that purpose. As the writesets have to be sent to all replicas, we use total order multicast for writeset dissemination. As outlined in Section 4.5, total order multicast guarantees that the writesets are delivered at all replicas in the same order, and we require the middleware replicas to perform validation in this order. By validating transactions at all replicas in the same order, we can ensure that all make the same decisions about commit or abort of transactions.

7.4.1 PROTOCOL DESCRIPTION

The decentralized protocol can be found in Figure 7.8. It has the same phases as in the protocol of the previous section.

Local phase. The client submits its transactions to any of the middleware replicas. Replica discovery, as discussed in Section 4.4, enables the client to find an available replica. With the first operation, a transaction receives its start timestamp (lines 3-4), and all read and write operations are executed at the local replica (lines 5-6). This concludes the local phase.

Validation phase. When the client submits the commit request the validation phase starts. A read-only transaction can commit immediately (lines 7-9). For update transactions, the transaction (including its writeset) is multicast in total order to all replicas (lines 11-12). Upon the delivery of the writeset, each replica performs the validation against previously validated transactions that were concurrent to the one being validated (line 13). If unsuccessful, the transaction is aborted at the local database (lines 14-16). If successful, the application phase starts.

Application phase. A remote replica first applies the writeset and then commits the transactions (lines 18-20). At the local replica, the transaction can immediately commit (line 20). The transaction is assigned a new commit timestamp, and the transaction is recorded for future validations (line 23). Finally, the local replica returns the confirmation to the client (lines 24-25).

The entire process after delivery of a writeset, i.e., validation, application of the writeset and commit is performed in a critical section. This means all writesets are applied sequentially, and the commit order reflects the validation order. Furthermore, starting a transaction (i.e., executing the first operation of a transaction in lines 5-6) must be synchronized with committing transactions and assigning commit timestamps (lines 20-22) to guarantee that the middleware has the correct start timestamp for a transaction. This can be achieved by setting appropriate mutexes.

Compared to the centralized execution, each replica only keeps track of its own commit and start timestamps. As validation and application phase are in a critical section, a single *lastcommitted* counter is sufficient for timestamping purposes.

Upon: Initialization
1: lastcommitted:=0
2: validateSet:= ∅

Upon: receiving operation of transaction T_i from a client
3:   **if** this is the first operation of T_i **then**
4:       T_i.startTS:=lastcommitted
5:   submit the operation to local database replica
6:   wait for response and return to client

Upon: receiving commit request for T_i from a client
7:   **if** T_i is read-only **then**
8:       commit at local database
9:       return confirmation to client
10: **else**
11:       Extract T_i's writeset WS_i from local database
12:       total_multicast T_i to all replicas

Upon: delivering transaction T_i in total order
13: **if** $\nexists T_j \in validateSet: (T_i.startTS < T_j.commitTS) \wedge (T_i.WS \cap T_j.WS \neq \emptyset)$ **then**
14:       **if** transaction local **then**
15:           abort T_i at local database
16:           send abort notification to client
17: **else**
18:       **if** transaction remote (from other replica) **then**
19:           apply WS_i at local database
20:       commit T_i at local database
21:       lastcommitted++
22:       T_i.commitTS:= lastcommitted
23:       append T_i to validateSet
24:       **if** transaction local **then**
25:           return confirmation to client

Figure 7.8: SI update anywhere protocol with decentralized middleware

7.4.2   EXAMPLE EXECUTION

The example uses the same five transactions as the previous examples. The execution at the two middleware replicas and corresponding database replicas is shown in Figure 7.9. For simplicity, the interaction between client and middleware replicas is omitted. We assume an initial transaction T_0 with commit timestamp 0 that created versions of all data items.

Transactions T_1, T_2 and T_5 are submitted to the middleware replica R^A while T_3 and T_4 are submitted to the middleware replica R^B. T_1 to T_4 receive 0 as start timestamp and execute

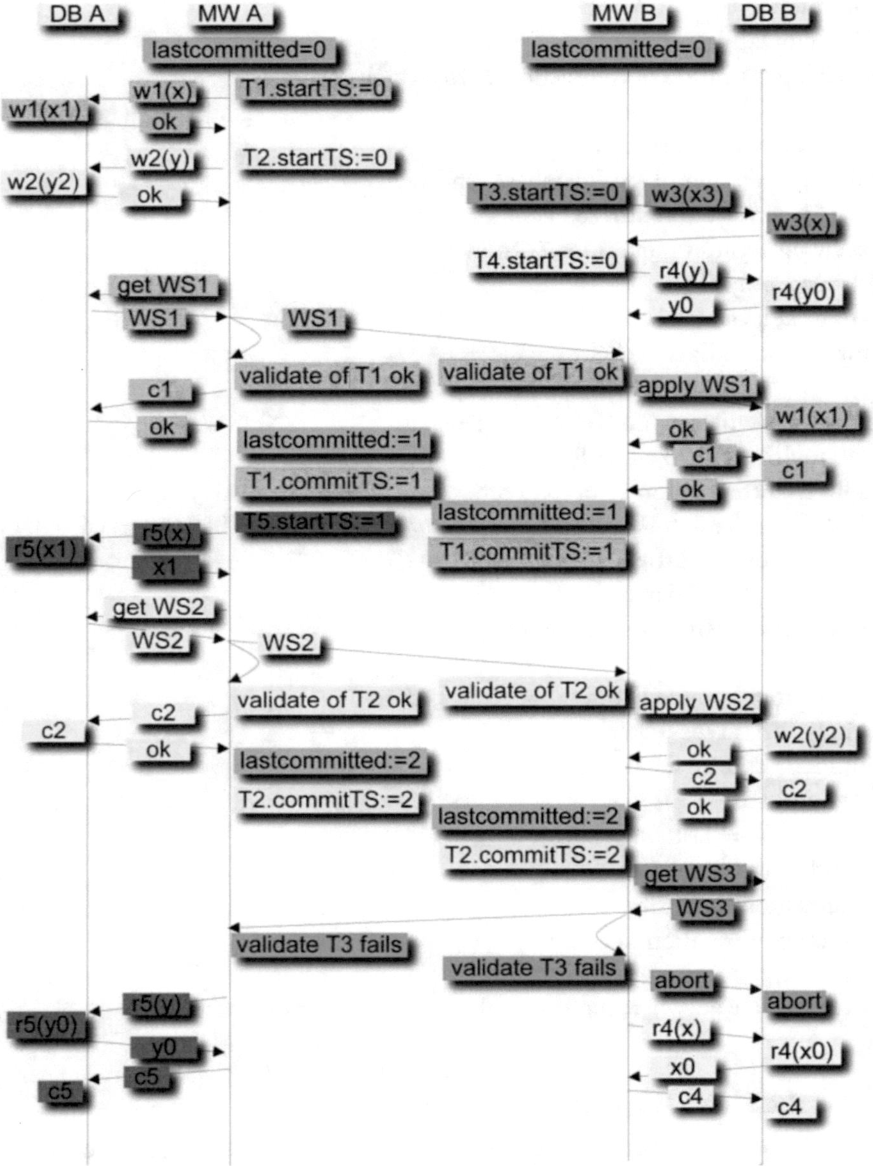

Figure 7.9: Example execution of SI update anywhere with decentralized middleware

their operations locally. We show the execution at R^A and R^B as overlapping because a clear order of operations cannot be determined if they execute on different replicas. When T_1 submits the commit request, the middleware of R^B retrieves the writeset and multicasts it in total order to all middleware replicas. Upon delivery, validation succeeds at both replicas, the middleware of R^B applies the writeset and both replicas commit the transaction. When T_5 starts at R^A, the middleware assigns a start timestamp of 1 as T_1 has already committed at the local database replica. T_2 commits in a similar way as T_1. The writeset is multicast and validation succeeds at both replicas as T_1 and T_2 do not conflict, and T_2 commits at both replicas. In contrast, the validation of T_3 fails. R^A simple discards the writeset while R^B has to abort the transaction at the local database replica. T_4 and T_5 finish their last read operations and also commit. Both read the initial version x_0 and y_0, respectively, as they read from a committed snapshot as of start time.

7.4.3 ALGORITHM PROPERTIES

1-copy-snapshot isolation. 1-copy-SI is achieved through three mechanisms. First, multicasting writesets in total order and validating them upon delivery guarantees that validation of all update transactions is performed in the same order at all replicas. Second, by validating update transactions in the same order, all replicas adopt the same commit/abort decisions. Third, total order, multicast also guarantees that update transactions are committed in the same order; at all replicas producing the same sequence of snapshots at all replicas.

The reasoning for properties (i) and (iii) of 1-copy-SI is the same as in the protocol of the previous section, and we omit it here. We only want to discuss the second property. All replicas commit the same set of update transactions because of the total order delivery of writesets and the resulting deterministic validation. Let us assume a simple example where T_1 and T_2 execute concurrently at two replicas and both update x. Without total order, it would be possible that one replica validates T_1 before T_2 and aborts T_2 while the other validates T_2 before T_1, and thus, aborts T_1. The second property of 1-copy-SI would be violated. But with total order delivery, all validate transactions in the same order; all abort the second transaction, which is the same at all replicas. The reasoning that a transaction will commit in the database when its middleware replica has successfully validated is again similar to the protocol of the previous section.

1-copy-atomicity. 1-copy-atomicity is trivially fulfilled in the failure-free case. Failures can be easily handled if we use uniform reliable multicast. It guarantees that whenever a writeset is delivered at any replica, it will be delivered at all available replicas, and thus, be processed by all. Therefore, if the failed replica has committed a transaction before the failure, all available replicas will do the same. A transaction that was local at the failed replica and whose writeset was not yet delivered was still active at the local replica when it failed. It can be considered aborted at all replicas. Therefore, 1-copy-atomicity is provided.

7.5   SNAPSHOT ISOLATION VS. TRADITIONAL OPTIMISTIC CONCURRENCY CONTROL

In this chapter, we assumed an implementation of snapshot isolation where conflicts between update transactions are detected at the end of transactions. This is the mechanism that basically all replica control protocols based on snapshot isolation use. Having a validation phase at the end of transaction is an optimistic concurrency control mechanism. Traditionally, however, optimistic concurrency control mechanisms were designed to provide serializability. The best known version is the Kung-Robinson model [Kung and Robinson, 1981]. In a local phase, a transaction reads the last committed version of a data item x, while write operations create versions that are only visible to the transaction itself. At the end of transaction, a validation phase checks whether each of the read versions still reflects the last committed version (i.e., there were no concurrent writes that are already validated). If yes, the commit phase turns the data item versions created by the transaction into visible versions. Otherwise, the transaction aborts, which simply means to discard its data item versions. As we have described the protocol here, it requires performing the validation and commit phases in a critical section.

In summary, most optimistic concurrency control mechanisms that provide serializability determine conflicts by checking for overlaps between readsets and writesets of concurrent transactions. Comparing this to the snapshot isolation implementation described in this chapter, the only difference is that snapshot isolation compares writesets against writesets. Therefore, the 1-copy-SI protocols that we described in this chapter could be easily adjusted to an optimistic concurrency control protocol providing 1-copy-serializability. The only major difference is that one has to collect also the readset of a transaction. For example, in protocol of Figure 7.8, if we could retrieve at line 7 not only the writeset but also the readset, we could multicast both sets to all replicas. Validation would then not check whether the writeset but whether the readset overlaps with the writeset of any concurrent validated transaction, and abort if this were the case.

7.6   RELATED WORK

The first work that exploits snapshot isolation in a replicated environment is Ganymed [Plattner and Alonso, 2004]. It uses a primary copy approach, and the primary copy protocol presented in Section 7.2 is a simplified version of Ganymed.

Several update anywhere approaches were proposed shortly after. Postgres-R(SI) [Wu and Kemme, 2005] integrates a replica control solution based on snapshot isolation into the kernel of the PostgreSQL database system. Conceptually, the approach taken is similar to the decentralized protocol described in Section 7.4. The version of PostgreSQL used for the work offers snapshot isolation based on a multi-version system. Posgres-R(SI) extends the system to be able to multicast writesets to all replicas using a total order multicast. Each replica performs validation. Different to the approaches presented here, however, PostgreSQL uses a locking mechanism that detects conflicts between writers during transaction execution and not at the end of transaction, and the replica control protocol is adjusted to work with this mechanism.

Lin et al. [2005] presents middleware based replication protocols, and the protocols presented here are variations of them. The difference is that the work described by Lin et al. [2005] uses PostgreSQL as underlying database system, and as mentioned above, it uses locking to detect write conflicts. This locking can lead to deadlocks between the replication logic and the database. This paper was the first one to characterize 1-copy-SI and prove that the protocol was 1-copy-SI.

Krikellas et al. [2010] propose a centralized middleware based approach that achieves what is named "strong consistency". After a transaction commits at any replica, a transaction that starts at a different replica is delayed until the changes of the committed replica have been applied at that replica. If the data items the transactions are going to access are known in advance, only the relevant data items have to be brought up-to-date.

A formal framework for reasoning about 1-copy-SI in replicated protocols was proposed by Lin et al. [2009]. Our discussion in Section 7.1.2 is derived from there. Generalized snapshot isolation (GS) [Elnikety et al., 2005] is a relaxation of SI. GSI enables read-only transaction to start on earlier snapshots than the current one. Daudjee and Salem [2006] propose different levels of SI, similar to 1-copy-SI and the more relaxed GSI for lazy replication. The proposed primary copy protocols forward updates automatically to the primary and enforce session consistency guaranteeing that clients observe their own writes. A further formalism of snapshot isolation in a replicated environment is introduced by Muñoz-Escoí et al. [2009].

Tashkent [Elnikety et al., 2006] uses GSI as correctness criteria and relies on a single validation component. Middleware replicas receive and execute transactions from clients. At the end of transaction, validation is performed by sending the necessary information to the certification component that decides on the validation order and performs validation. The validator can be replicated for fault-tolerance purposes.

Mishima and Nakamura [2009] propose a primary-secondary approach based on GSI. Secondaries commit update transactions in the same order as the primary. As all primary-secondary approaches, it assumes a priori knowledge about transactions being read-only or update transactions.

SI has also be analyzed in the context of partial replication [Bernabé-Gisbert et al., 2008; Serrano et al., 2007]. The challenges are to perform validation although replicas do not have all copies, and to provide transactions a single global snapshot if they access data copies on different nodes.

Finally, SI has also been exploited in multi-tier systems using SI databases [Perez-Sorrosal et al., 2007]. Interestingly enough, a regular J(2)EE application server when used in combination with an SI database violates SI. The reason is that application servers cache data from the database, but they have a single version cache. This means that if there are two transactions requiring two different snapshots from the same data item that is cached at the application server, only one of them might receive the right version of the item. Perez-Sorrosal et al. [2007] propose a multi-version cache for the application server that provides end-to-end SI consistency. The authors also present a protocol for replicating the multi-tier system by collocating an application server and a database as a single replication unit and encapsulating the replication logic in the application server.

CHAPTER 8

Lazy Replication

In this chapter, we have a closer look at lazy protocols. Lazy protocols execute transactions first locally and only send the update information some time after commit. In primary copy approaches, this means that the primary always has the current version of the data item while secondary copies might be stale. In Section 8.1, we present mechanisms that quantify and bound the staleness that can be observed at the secondaries. In Section 8.2, we discuss how lazy primary copy approaches can be made more flexible by allowing the primary copies to be distributed across many replicas. Section 8.3 is dedicated to lazy update anywhere approaches. The particular problem of this protocol category is that transactions executing on different replicas can concurrently update the same data items and all commit. We present mechanisms that allow the detection of such conflicts, and we discuss strategies that resolve these conflicts in order to agree on a final value for the corresponding data items.

8.1   BOUNDING THE STALENESS IN LAZY PRIMARY COPY

Section 3.2 presented a lazy primary copy replica control algorithm where read-only transactions can be submitted to any replica and execute completely locally at this replica. An update transaction executes and commits first at the primary. Only "some time after the commit" the changes of transactions are propagated to the secondary replicas. At the secondaries, the changes are applied in the order in which they committed at the primary. The protocol provides 1-copy-serializability, but read-only transactions on the secondaries might read stale data. How stale, is not defined, and readers at the secondaries do not know how outdated the copies really are. In this section, we discuss how the staleness of secondary copies can be bound.

The best one can do is to send the updates immediately after commit and apply them at the remote replicas as soon as they arrive. In this situation, the maximum staleness is the time for the update transfer. However, that can be costly, and it might not be needed if readers can live with staler data. Therefore, many approaches provide more relaxed guarantees.

8.1.1   BOUNDARY TYPES

The main definitions to bound staleness are based on time, value, and update frequency.

- A system offers *time-bound staleness* with time limit t for a data item x if a secondary copy is stale for at most t time units. This means that if a write operation $w(x)$ setting x to a value a occurs at the primary copy at time point TP, then at $TP + t$ all secondary copies of x either have the value a or a value of a write operation that occurred after $w(x)$. For instance, assume a time bound of one hour for data item x. Further assume the primary copy of x is changed from 0 to 1 at 14:20, and then at 14:40 it is set to 2. At 15:20 the latest, all secondary copies should have either the value 1 (reflecting the first update) or 2 (already reflecting the second update).

- A system offers *value-based staleness* if the values of the secondary copies never differ from the value at the primary copy by more than a predefined *threshold difference*. Value-based staleness limits the value drift between primary and secondary copy. Of course, such a bound is only possible if a difference function is defined on the data type of the data item. The threshold difference can be defined in absolute or percentage values. For instance, assume a data item of type integer and an absolute value bound of 5. Further assume a data item x has the same value 2 at all replicas, and then the primary copy is first changed to 4 and then to 8. At latest, when the primary changes to 8, either the secondaries have the value 4 (reflecting the first update) or 8 (reflecting both updates). As a second example, assume a percentage bound of 10% and the current value of data item x is 100 at all copies. A change to 105 will not require any propagation, but once the value changes above 110 or below 90, propagation needs to be triggered.

- A system offers *update-based staleness* if the updates missed by the secondaries are limited by an *update threshold*. With an update threshold of 1, each update on the primary copy has to be immediately propagated to the secondaries. With a threshold of 2, when the second update occurs at the primary, the secondaries need to receive at least the first update.

8.1.2   BASIC IMPLEMENTATION

Staleness bounds have first been developed without the concept of transactions in mind. Instead, they are defined on each data item individually, not taking into consideration that a transaction might update several data items and that these updates should be considered a logical unit. Therefore, we ignore transactions for now and purely focus on achieving the desired staleness level. This means that update transactions execute and commit at the primary without any writeset being collected. Instead, the primary simply keeps track of when data items are updated. When the staleness bound of a data item is reached, the current value of the data item is propagated to the secondaries. We discuss the impact on transactions in the next section. For all staleness types, the primary copy is tagged with additional information that helps to decide when to propagate.

- *Time-bound Staleness:* Assume a data item x has a time-bound of t. Whenever the primary copy of x is updated, and the primary copy is not yet tagged, it receives the current time TP_1 as timestamp. If it is tagged, nothing extra is done. At time point $TP_1 + t$, the current value of the primary copy is propagated to the secondaries, and the primary copy is untagged.

    As an example, assume all copies of x have the same value 0. Then, the primary copy of x is changed from 0 to 1 at 14:20, and then at 14:40 it is set to 2. At the time of the first update, the primary copy is tagged with a timestamp 14:20. The second update finds a timestamp tag and does not need to do anything special. At 15:20, the current value of the primary copy, i.e., 2, is propagated to the secondaries, fulfilling the time-bound for both updates. After the propagation the timestamp is removed, and a new one is only added with the next update.

- *Value-based Staleness:* The primary copy is tagged with the difference of its current value and the values at the secondaries. Whenever the difference is larger than the threshold difference, the primary propagates its current value to the secondaries.

  For instance, assume a threshold difference of 5, and all copies of a data item x have the value 2. Thus, the primary copy is tagged with the difference 0. When the primary copy is updated to 4, it is tagged with the difference $4 - 2 = 2$. When a second update changes the primary to 8, the difference changes to 6, triggering the propagation of the current value 8 to all secondaries.

- *Update-based Staleness:* The primary copy is tagged with the number of updates that the secondaries miss. When all copies have incorporated the same updates, the tag is 0, and it is incremented by 1 every time an update occurs. If the tag is equal to the update threshold, the current value of the data item is propagated to the secondaries and the tag reset to 0. An update threshold of 1 forces every update to be propagated.

An interesting aspect of this implementation is that not necessarily every single update is propagated. The example illustrating time-bound staleness, for instance, updates data item x twice within the time bound t, but only one transfer is necessary.

Several bounds per data item.   It might be possible that every secondary has a different bound for a given data item. For instance, if there are copies in the same local area network and in remote networks, one might want to keep the local secondary as consistent as possible as update propagation is cheap, while the remote secondaries have a looser bound. This can be implemented by keeping at the primary a tag per secondary copy.

8.1.3   PUSH VS. PULL BASED REFRESH

What we have described so far is push-based update propagation, as the primary pushes the changes to the secondaries whenever the bounds are reached. Push-based approaches are by far the most common for replication. A pull-based approach is also possible. In this case, the secondaries ask the primary for a new version of the data item instead of the primary actively pushing it. A pull-based approach might be interesting if the secondary copy is rarely accessed, i.e., there are much fewer reads on the secondary copy than there are writes on the primary. Pulling is frequently used in caching approaches when a time-based staleness bound has to be guaranteed. A secondary copy has the timestamp TP_1 of when it was propagated from the primary copy. As long as the current time is less than TP_1 plus the time-boundary t, the local copy is guaranteed to fulfill the bound. At $TP_1 + t$ or some time after (e.g., when a request for the data item arrives), the secondary makes a pull-request to the primary to see whether the primary copy has changed. If the primary returns a negative answer, the timestamp of the secondary copy can be set to the current time, and it is valid for at least another t units. Otherwise, the primary can send the new value to the secondary. Further optimizations are possible. Value- and update-based staleness limits cannot be achieved with such a pull-based approach as the secondary has no means to know how often the primary copy is changed, or to what value it is set.

8.1.4   MATERIALIZED VIEWS

Lazy primary copy replication has similarities with materialized views. A materialized view reflects the results of a query (e.g., an SQL query) that is possibly defined over several tables. The results are not computed every time the view is called, but the query is executed once and the result stored as materialized view. Thus, a materialized view is a read-only copy of the original data, but it does not have the same schema as the base data. Most commercial systems offer such functionality. When the base tables change, the materialized view has to be updated. This can be done by reexecuting the complete query, which is often necessary when the query is complex and covers more than one table. For rather simple queries, it is possible to incrementally update the view as changes to individual records occur.

8.1.5   TRANSACTION PROPAGATION

We already mentioned that the implementations presented so far ignore transactions. Transactions can update several data items. It is now possible that each data item has a different bound, leading to different propagation times, and thus, to possible non-serializable reads at the secondaries. For instance, assume a transaction updates both x and y, the change on x is propagated at time TP_1 and the change on y at $TP_2 > TP_1$. If a read-only transaction reads x and y at a time TP_3, $TP_1 < TP_3 < TP_2$, then execution is no longer serializable as it sees the update on x but not the update on y. A possible solution is to take the minimum bound on any of the data items to propagate all data items that were changed by a transaction. That means, whenever a data item is updated, the system keeps track of the transaction performing the update. Then, when the new value of a data item is scheduled to be propagated, all other data items that were updated by that transaction are also propagated. Note that this can have a cascading affect. For instance, transaction T_1 updates x and y, and T_2 later updates y and z. Propagating x requires propagating y, but as the last change on y was done by T_2, it requires propagating z, too. Such a scheme can become complex and requires the calculation of a transitive closure.

Therefore, some approaches do not require a completely consistent snapshot at the secondaries. Instead, they guarantee a maximum drift between the different data items. For instance, if a transaction reads both x and y, a drift limit of 1 second provides the guarantee that the versions read are within 1 second of each other.

Alternatively and in order to provide serializable execution for read-only transactions on secondaries, many systems propagate updates on a transaction basis similar to what we have described in Section 3.2. Figure 8.1 presents the protocol in simplified form focusing on the writeset propaga-

Upon: $r_i(x)$ for local transaction T_i

1: execute operation locally

Upon: $w_i(x)$ for local transaction T_i {only allow at primary replica}

2: execute operation locally

3: collect in writeset WS_i

Upon: commit request for local transaction T_i

4: commit T_i

5: enqueue non-empty WS_i in writeset FIFO queue Q

Upon: staleness bound for data item x reached

6: let WS_i be writeset so that, if applied at secondary, staleness bound is recovered

7: send all writesets in Q up to WS_i in FIFO order to secondary replicas

Upon: *receiving writeset WS_i from primary*

8: apply writeset in receiving order

Figure 8.1: Bounded update propagation

tion. During transaction execution, a writeset is collected (lines 2-3). At commit time, the writeset is queued (lines 4-5). In order to allow for different staleness bounds, the propagation itself might be delayed depending on the staleness limits (lines 6-7), but it is on a transaction basis. The staleness limits only determine the latest time point a writeset has to be propagated. That is, if a data item is updated several times within the defined staleness bound, not only the final value, but each individual update is propagated to the secondaries. The writesets are applied at the secondaries in the order the transactions committed at the primary (line 8) guaranteeing that read-only transactions at secondaries read from a transaction consistent snapshot.

For instance, if a data item x has a time bound t, we can tag a writeset containing x with t and the time TP_1 at which the writeset was produced. The writeset then needs to be propagated at the latest at $TP_1 + t$. As another example, assume a data item x has value-based staleness with threshold difference of 5. If x is first changed from 2 to 4, and then later to 8, the writeset containing the first update has to be sent the latest after the second update has executed at the primary (guaranteeing that the difference between secondary and primary is $8 - 4 < 5$). If x changes from 2 directly to 8, then this update has to be propagated immediately. Finally, for update-based staleness, whenever a secondary misses more than the predefined threshold of updates, the writeset with the oldest update has to be propagated.

Of course, if updates are propagated in form of writesets and applied in commit order, it is quite likely that updates are sent ahead of time. For example, assume a transaction updates x and y, and x has a time-bound staleness of 1 hour, while y has one of 2 hours. The writeset will be sent the latest one hour after the transaction commits due to the bound on x. Thus, for y the update arrives well ahead of time.

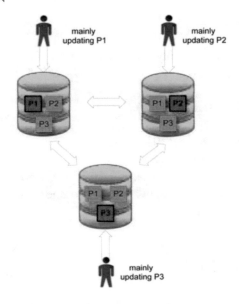

Figure 8.2: Multiple replicas with primary copies

8.2   MULTIPLE PRIMARIES

Having a single node that has the primary copies of all data items can lead to a bottleneck for update transactions. Furthermore, clients that are remote to this primary experience long response times for all of their update transactions. Having multiple primary nodes can alleviate this problem. Often, a database can be partitioned by regions (e.g., all clients from a certain region and the related data belong to one partition). Clients that belong to a certain region typically access more often the data that can be associated to that region rather than to other regions. For instance, taking the puppet store from the introduction, assume that the store has warehouses in many regions, and the company installs a replica of its database at each of these warehouses. Clients will connect to the local warehouse of their regions. They will mainly access their own client information and the pricing and stock information of their particular warehouse. They might, however, also access globally valid data, such as general product information, etc. Thus, the idea is that the replica residing in a region hosts the primary copies for the corresponding partition. With this, clients have close access to the primary copies of the data they are most interested in, resulting in faster update transactions. This scenario is depicted in Figure 8.2. The database is partitioned into partitions $P1$, $P2$, $P3$, and the primary copies of these partitions are depicted in bold.

Transaction execution.   Read-only transactions can be submitted to any replica and execute locally. Update transactions can read any data item but are only allowed to update data items that belong

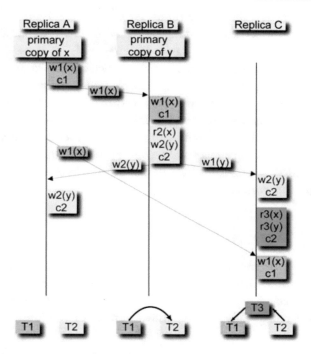

Figure 8.3: Unserializable execution with multiple primaries

to a single partition. Updates across two partitions are not possible because two different replicas hold their primary copies. Thus, the choice of partitions needs to be well adjusted according to the different transaction types that exist in the application. Ideally, most update transactions for a partition are submitted by clients that are local to the primary copy of the partition, avoiding communication across wide area links.

Primary copy placement and serializability.   Using multiple primary nodes seems a straightforward extension to a single primary replica, and it has its obvious advantages in a wide area setting. In regard to consistency, however, some subtle issues arise. In particular, 1-copy-serializability is no longer provided, even if the replication protocol follows the description in Section 3.2, where all updates of a transaction are sent in a single writeset and applied at the secondaries as an atomic unit. Let us look at a simple example as depicted in Figure 8.3. Assume a database consisting of two data items x and y where x's primary copy resides on replica R^A, and y's primary copy is on replica R^B. Now assume a transaction T_1 executes at R^A updating x. The change is propagated to R^B and R^C. At R^B, T_2 reads the freshly updated x, writes y, and commits. The change is propagated to R^A and R^C. At R^C, T_2's update arrives first and is applied. Then a transaction T_3 reads the new value of y

but still the old value of x as T_1's update arrives late. At R^B, the serialization graph is $T_1 \rightarrow T_2$, as T_2 reads T_1's update. At R^C, the serialization graph is $T_2 \rightarrow T_3 \rightarrow T_1$, due to the read-dependencies of T_3. Taking the union of both graphs, we have a cycle $T_1 \rightarrow T_2 \rightarrow T_3 \rightarrow T_1$. The problem is that T_2's update depends on an update of T_1, but T_3 only sees one of the two updates.

One has to note that this is a very specific example, and in many cases, such situations might never arise. However, this example also shows quite nicely that seemingly straightforward techniques such as distributing primary copies can have subtle implications for the correctness of algorithms. In fact, providing 1-copy-serializability in multi-primary environments is not straightforward. Some solutions restrict the placement of primary and secondary copies; others introduce complex coordination algorithms to achieve serializability. We do not discuss them in detail here but only point to some of them in the related work section.

8.3   LAZY UPDATE ANYWHERE

Lazy update anywhere allows any copy of a data item to be updated. As transactions first commit locally without coordination with other replicas, concurrent updates of two copies of the same data item can only be detected and resolved after transaction commit. Detecting such conflicts and resolving them are challenging. This section outlines how it can be addressed.

8.3.1   DISTRIBUTED VS. CENTRAL CONFLICT MANAGEMENT

Section 3.2 presents a lazy update anywhere protocol with distributed conflict management, as every replica detects and resolves conflicts locally. However, it can also be done in a centralized fashion. In a centralized architecture, there is only one node or replica that detects and resolves conflicts and tells the others what to do. This architecture is often chosen if there is a special node that has a more central role in the replication architecture. For instance, there is one central database and the other replicas exist, e.g., on mobile or personal computers, that could be easily disconnected. In this environment, a primary copy approach is not suitable, as communication to the primary might be slow or not available at all, hindering the execution of update transactions. In contrast, an update anywhere approach allows all update transactions to be local. Nevertheless, the central unit can be given the authority of conflict detection and resolution, and probably also update propagation. The idea is that a replica sends changes only to the central unit and not to all replicas. The central unit checks for possible conflicts and resolves them if necessary. It then propagates all successfully executed changes to the other replicas, which can apply them blindly.

Having a single authority simplifies conflict resolution as it automatically guarantees determinism. In contrast, with distributed conflict management every replica receives all updates independently and has to locally detect and resolve the conflicts. As replicas receive updates from different nodes possibly in different order neither conflict detection nor deterministic resolution are trivial.

8.3.2 CONFLICT DETECTION

Three types of conflicts can occur. A *uniqueness conflict* happens when two inserts attempt to insert a data item with the same unique identifier (i.e., the same primary key in SQL). An *update conflict* happens when two concurrent transactions update the same data item. A *delete conflict* happens when one transaction deletes a data item that another transaction updates or deletes.

Conflict detection with central conflict management. With central conflict management, conflict detection is quite easy. Whenever the central unit updates its copy of a data item, it receives a new version, and that version number is propagated together with the changed value. When another replica applies this change to its local copy, it also keeps track of the version number. When a replica now sends a new change to the central unit, it tags it with the current version of the copy that it has locally. At the central unit, upon receiving such an update, it compares the version of the received update with the version of its local copy. If they are the same, then no other replica has concurrently updated that data item yet, and there is no conflict. The update is applied and a new version is created. But if the local version is larger than the piggybacked version, another replica has updated the data item and that update was received earlier by the central unit. Conflict resolution is triggered. If the value of the data item changes due to the resolution (see next section), a new version number is created for the item.

Conflict detection with distributed conflict management. Such simple version numbers cannot be used with distributed conflict management because each replica needs to create versions locally making it difficult to have globally coherent versions. For instance, assume a transaction updates x at replica R^A, and another transaction updates x at replica R^B. If each replica has version 100 before the execution, the version will be 101 at both replicas after the execution. Conflict detection and resolution at both replicas has to establish deterministically the correct version after resolution is completed. Will it be 101 or maybe 102? If more than two concurrent transactions exist, globally correct version numbers quickly become difficult to achieve.

A common approach to versioning updates in a distributed system is the use of *version vectors*[1]. Version vectors are similar in concept to vector clocks [Mattern, 1989]. A version vector for a data item contains a version entry for each replica in the system. The copy of the data item at replica R^i is tagged with version vector V_i. The entries of the vector reflect the versions that are already incorporated in the copy. When a replica R^i updates its copy, it increases its own version entry $V_i[i]$. Not only the update itself but also the corresponding version vector is included in the writeset. When another replica R^j receives an update from replica R^i, it can detect whether there was any concurrent update by comparing the version vector V_i included in the writeset with its local version vector V_j for that data item. If $V_i[i] = V_j[i] + 1$ and for all other k, $k \neq i$, $V_i[k] = V_j[k]$, then there is no conflict. If for some $k \neq i$, $V_i[k] > V_j[k]$, the replica R^j is missing some updates that R^i has already seen. It can delay R^i's update until it receives these missing updates. If, however, there

---

[1] In general, vectors are very common to relate and order events in a distributed system.

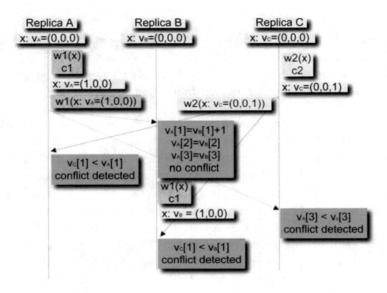

Figure 8.4: Distributed conflict detection with version vectors

is some $k \neq i$ such that $V_i[k] < V_j[k]$, then there is a conflict between transactions on R^i and R^k. Conflict resolution is needed.

Figure 8.4 shows an example with replicas R^A, R^B and R^C. All copies of data item x have version vectors (0,0,0). At R^A and R^C, T_1 and T_2 concurrently update x, leading to version vectors $V_A = (1, 0, 0)$ and $V_C = (0, 0, 1)$. When R^A receives T_2's update a conflict is detected as $V_C[1] < V_A[1]$, i.e., the update from T_1 was not yet incorporated in the copy of R^C when T_2's update at R^C occurred. At R^C, the conflict is detected in a similar way when the update from T_1 arrives. Now assume that at R^B, T_1's update arrives first. No conflict is detected as $V_A[1] = V_B[1] + 1$, and all other entries are the same. The update is applied and V_B set to $(1, 0, 0)$. When now T_2's update arrives, the conflict is detected in the same way as at R^A.

From a conceptual point of view, version vectors are a very powerful and elegant tool. The problem with version vectors is that the size can become quite large if there are many replicas in the system. Having such a large version vector for each data item in the system quickly becomes unfeasible. Also, if replicas can join and leave dynamically, vector maintenance is a challenge.

In fact, many commercial systems do not use any versioning at all. Instead, they send with each update on data item x, both the before- and after-image of x. Instead of using version numbers to detect conflicts, the before-image sent in a write-set message is compared with the current value of the data item. If they are the same, no concurrent updates are assumed. If they are different, a conflict is detected.

8.3.3   CONFLICT RESOLUTION

Once conflict detection has determined that two transactions updated concurrently the same data item, conflict resolution has to determine a final value for the data item. The final goal is *eventual consistency* as defined in Section 2.8. The idea is that all copies of a data item will eventually converge to the same value once no updates have occurred for a sufficiently long time. Of course, as long as updates occur, it might always be the case that some of the copies are out of date. But once the system is in a quiescent state, the copies should converge. Eventual consistency is not transaction aware and looks at each data item individually. As a result, if two concurrent transactions T_1 and T_2 update x and y, it might happen that after conflict detection and resolution, x has the value written by T_1 and y has the value written by T_2.

For update conflicts, there exist many resolution mechanisms. Some are general, others depend on the data type.

1. General resolution mechanisms

   - *Discard.* When a conflicting update arrives, it is simply discarded and the local value is not changed. This mechanism provides eventual consistency only if there is a central conflict detection and resolution unit. If resolution is done in a distributed fashion, copies will quickly diverge. Just looking at the example of Figure 8.4, if replicas simply discard the last update they receive, R^A and R^B will have T_1's update while R^C will have T_2's update. The copies differ after resolution.

   - *Overwrite.* When a conflicting update arrives, it overwrites the local value. That is, *over-write* is the opposite of *discard*, and again only provides eventual consistency with a central resolution unit.

   - *Site priority.* Each replica in the replicated system must be given a priority in advance. The resolution method chooses the value of the replica with the highest priority. In the example of Figure 8.4, assume R^A has higher priority than R^C. Then R^A and R^B will discard the update from T_2 as it originates from lower priority replica R^C. In contrast, R^C will apply T_1's update because R^A has higher priority. At the end, all copies have the value of x written by T_1. Interestingly, convergence is not guaranteed in all cases. In particular, if detection is done using before- and after-images, and if propagation delays are frequent, situations can arise where copies can diverge. We leave it to the interested reader to come up with such an example.

   - *Value priority.* Assuming there is a mechanism to give each possible value of the data item a priority, then given the two values produced by two conflicting updates, the value with the higher priority wins. For instance, if a data item can take the values *ordered, produced, shipped, delivered*, then priorities $ordered < produced < shipped < delivered$ could be assigned, as this reflects the order in which the values for this data item will typically change.

- *Timestamp priority*. Each data item is tagged with a timestamp that could reflect the local time when the update takes place. Ideally, the timestamp is so fine-grained that global uniqueness is provided. In case of a conflict, the value with either the earliest or latest timestamp can be taken, the other discarded. Section 3.2 discusses for the example in Figure 3.6 largest timestamp as a possible resolution mechanism.

2. Data-type specific resolution mechanisms are mainly designed for numerical data types or types that have a comparison operation.

- *Minimum/maximum* takes the smallest/largest value of conflicting updates.
- *Additive* assumes that the update itself is an addition or subtraction. For example, given a data item x with current value 100, and transaction T_1 on replica R^A increases the value to 105 (basically adding 5), and T_2 on replica R^B increases it to 110 (adding 10). In principle, these transactions are commutative. Thus, it is straightforward to come up with a final solution that is equivalent to a serial execution. When T_2's update (with before-image 100 and after-image 110) arrives, and the local value of 105 is detected, then the final value is set to the local value plus the after-image minus the before-image: 105 + (110-100). The result is 115, which would also be the result if both transactions had executed serially, one after the other. Note that as soon as several operation types are possible on the same data item (e.g., multiplication and addition), such mechanism will not work anymore.

Uniqueness conflicts, where concurrent transactions insert data items with the same unique identifier, can be either avoided or resolved. A first avoidance mechanism is to have an identifier consisting of two values, a counter and a node identifier. Then each replica receives a unique node identifier and can produce counter values that only need to be locally unique. The combination of counter and node identifier is then globally unique. An alternative avoidance mechanism is to regularly provide each replica a range of available identifier values. Each time a new data item is created, the replica chooses one of the values assigned to it. The resolving mechanisms are a subset of those for update resolution, such as discard, overwrite, site priority and earliest/latest timestamp.

Many commercial systems allow application programmers to provide specific resolution programs that can be plugged into the resolution module. When a conflict occurs, the resolution program receives all available information (version numbers, current, before- and after-images) and can deploy an application specific reconciliation strategy. As a final mechanism, the system can simply throw an exception every time a conflict occurs and inform a management component. Further updates on the data item will be disallowed until explicitly reactivated after manual reconciliation.

8.4 RELATED WORK

8.4.1 BOUNDING STALENESS

The discussion of relaxed consistency guarantees started with the development of the first replicated databases [Alonso et al., 1990; Krishnakumar and Bernstein, 1991; Pu and Leff, 1991]. Quasi-copies [Alonso et al., 1990] discusses time-, value-, and update-bound staleness. Furthermore, they introduce periodic-bound staleness which requires secondaries to be refreshed in regular time intervals. They also discuss the problem of integrity constraint violations if updates on different data items are propagated at different times. While such constraints (e.g., the sum of two data items may not be below a certain value) always hold at the primary, due to missing updates at the secondaries, the constraint might be violated at the secondaries. The problem can be avoided by guaranteeing that changes are propagated in the order they were committed at the primary. Epsilon-serializability [Pu and Leff, 1991] defines a limit per transaction instead of per data item. A transaction defines a single threshold (e.g., update- or value-based) and then the sum of all staleness values over all data items read may not exceed this limit. The concept of bounded ignorance [Krishnakumar and Bernstein, 1991] also defines staleness in a transactional context by limiting the number of prior transactions whose results are not visible.

In Pacitti and Simon [2000], secondaries can either apply updates immediately when they receive it or later, whatever might be more efficient. Daudjee and Salem [2004] achieve session consistency by letting read-only transactions of clients only access data at secondaries that contain the last changes of this client.

Yu and Vahdat [2002] define error limits to a semantically defined conit instead of individual data items. The system does not support transactions. Various bounds are considered, such as time-, value- and order-bounds, where the latter refers to the number of updates that arrive at the secondaries in a different order than originally executed. Several types of bounds can be defined at the same time on a conit, and all bounds must be obeyed. Olston et al. [2001] offer a combined pull/push approach. Based on value-based staleness, as soon as the true value at the primary copy differs by more than the threshold difference from the secondary copy, the primary pushes the new value to the secondary copy. At the same time, if a client that accesses the secondary requires a tighter threshold difference than provided by the secondary copy, the secondary copy pulls the current value from the primary. Query-initiated pull is also proposed by Röhm et al. [2002]. Read-only transactions indicate the level of time-bound staleness they are willing to accept and the secondaries pull updates from the primary depending on the staleness levels indicated by their queries. Both the Leganet System [Gançarski et al., 2007] and DBFarm [Plattner et al., 2006b] have a central router that sends queries to replicas that have an acceptable staleness level. Akal et al. [2005] provide time-bound staleness guarantees. They also allow for flexible partial replication as it is possible that a read-only transaction executes at multiple nodes depending on which data items it accesses. Guo et al. [2004] provide an extension to SQL that allows the specification of time-based threshold values, and guarantees read-only queries that access one or more tables to retrieve data from a consistent snapshot. Bernstein et al. [2006] extend the approach to update transactions and other staleness criteria. Update transactions can submit their read requests to secondary copies where they might read stale but bounded data. The updates themselves are submitted and executed at the primary.

8.4.2   REPLICA PLACEMENT

The subtle problems of 1-copy-serializability in multi-master systems are introduced by Chundi et al. [1996]. Their solution is to restrict the location of primary and secondary copies. They assume a partial replication model where not all nodes have a full copy of the database but only copies of some of the data items. Then, for each data item, a node is chosen that holds the primary copy and a set of nodes that hold secondary copies. If the configuration does not show any circular behavior then execution can offer 1-copy-serializability. For instance, if one node holds the primary copy of x and the secondary copy of y, and another node holds the primary of y and the secondary of x, then there would be a cycle in the configuration which could possibly lead to non-serializable executions. The restrictions on copy location can be relaxed if more sophisticated update propagation strategies are used that guarantee that updates arrive in certain order at the different replicas [Breitbart et al., 1999; Pacitti et al., 1999].

8.4.3   CONFLICT DETECTION AND RESOLUTION

Within the database community, lazy update anywhere mechanisms have not received a lot of attention in the recent past. However, basically all commercial database systems provide them and offer a wide range of detection and resolution mechanisms as described in this chapter. Several distributed file systems, such as Coda [Kistler and Satyanarayanan, 1992] and Bayou [Terry et al., 1995], apply the ideas of lazy update anywhere and propose various conflict resolution mechanisms. Epidemic algorithms attempt to achieve eventual consistency in systems with large number of replicas [Malkhi and Terry, 2007; Rabinovich et al., 1996; Wang and Amza, 2009]. Version management, in particular the handling of version vectors, is an important aspect. A good overview is presented by Saito and Shapiro [2005].

CHAPTER 9

Self-Configuration and Elasticity

A replicated system is rarely static. First of all, the number of database replicas can change at any time. Replicas fail and need to be reintegrated into the system, or they need to be added or removed in order to provide the right amount of replicas for the given workload. Furthermore, as the workload and the number of replicas change, the load has to be distributed appropriately over the available replicas, Ideally, these reconfigurations occur *dynamically*, without interrupting current execution across the system, and *autonomous*, i.e., without too much manual intervention. Such autonomous and dynamic behavior can be expressed through *self-properties*.

In this chapter, we talk about three self-properties:

- *Self-healing* allows the system to properly handle failures, and consists of three different steps. First, during normal processing, when no failures occur, coordination protocols ensure that all components in the system have enough information to handle the failure of some of them. These protocols are mainly the *replica control protocols* that we have described in the previous chapters. Second, when a component fails, a *failover procedure* distributes the load assigned to the failed component to available replicas. Third, a failed component has to perform a *recovery procedure* in order to be reintegrated into the system. In the context of data replication, there are two main challenges: the data copies on the recovering replica have to be brought up to date as data might have changed during its downtime; furthermore, this recovery procedure should not interrupt execution in the remaining system, at least not for a long time. Bringing a database replica up-to-date could take a long time. It is essential that the remainder of the system is still functional during this time.

- *Self-optimization* refers to measures that aim at optimizing the performance of the existing system. We discuss some of them, such as load-balancing and replica placement.

- *Self-provisioning* is the task that decides on the right number of replicas in the system. In newer terminology, this is called *elasticity*. An elastic system is able to dynamically adjust its capacity to the current needs. Self-provisioning has to be able to add and remove replicas as needed. It can use variations of the self-healing failover and recovery procedures to do so.

9.1   SELF-HEALING

As discussed before, a self-healing system has to implement three different tasks: coordination during normal processing, failover, and recovery. Let us have a closer look at each of them.

9.1.1   FAULT-TOLERANT MEASURES DURING NORMAL PROCESSING

Replica control protocols during normal processing are used to keep the replicas consistent so that no matter where transactions access data, they see an acceptable state. Even if a replication solution is only implemented for fault-tolerance, i.e., all requests go to a primary and a backup replica will only be used in case of primary failure, the backup needs to know about all updates. Thus, we refer to the different protocols described in the previous chapters and use them as a baseline when we discuss failover and recovery. As mentioned before, lazy update propagation does not provide the same consistency level as eager approaches. Nevertheless, both eager and lazy approaches are used for high-availability solutions providing a trade-off between performance during normal processing and consistency in the case of a failover.

9.1.2   FAILURE TYPES

We can distinguish between various failure types. In this book, we only look at a very restricted type of failure, namely *process or machine crash*. In both cases, we assume that the particular replica stops execution of any tasks and does not communicate anymore with other replicas. All content stored in main memory is lost, while data on secondary storage survive the crash and can be accessed when the process/machine is restarted. This failure model is also referred to as crash-recovery model.

Network failures are very common, too, but we do not consider them in this chapter. Possible failure types are *network partitions, message loss* and *message corruption*. Especially in wide area settings, communication links might be broken such that all replicas are up but cannot communicate with each other for a considerable time. Quorums, which are shortly discussed in Chapter 10, can handle such partitions. In contrast, in this section, we assume that any partitions are only short-lived and will eventually be repaired. Message loss is often caused by restricted buffer sizes at the end nodes or intermediate routers, but it can be fairly easily handled by retransmission protocols (e.g., TCP). Similar, message corruption can be handled with checksums and retransmission mechanisms. Thus, we do not consider any of these failures but assume that point-to-point communication is reliable, i.e., each message sent is eventually received unless sender or receiver fail.

Finally, we assume that no *byzantine behavior* occurs where nodes perform actions that do not conform to the described protocols, be it due to software errors or malicious intentions. Byzantine failures make fault-tolerance considerably more complex. We refer the interested reader to Vandiver et al. [2007] for a broader discussion on this topic.

9.1.3   FAILOVER: CLIENT SIDE

Failover is the process through which the system reconfigures to overcome a failure of any of its components. There are two failover components, one runs at the client side, the other at the server side. In this section, we discuss the client side.

Client failover.   Clients typically connect to a database system through a standard database API, such as a JDBC or an ODBC driver. It is the client-side driver that provides the user the interface to submit queries and then marshals and sends these requests to the database system, receives the responses and returns them to the client in a language-conform format.

If replication should be transparent to the client, this driver has to be adjusted to perform any replication related tasks in a transparent manner. In particular, the driver hides the failure of a replica or the middleware from the real client. The driver typically communicates with the middleware or a replica via a connection. If the middleware/replica fails, the connection is broken. The next time the driver sends a request over the connection, it receives a failure message. This allows the driver to detect the failure and initiate the *client failover* in order to hide the failure from the client. The first task is to find an available replica or the backup middleware and connect to it. The second task is to resubmit the last request over the new connection, i.e., the request for which a failure exception was received as response.

Replica discovery.   The client must find a new replica or middleware in order to automatically reconnect after failure. Such information can be requested explicitly at failover or maintained at run-time. In the first case, replica discovery can be used such as it was done when the client first connected to the system (see Chapter 4). Replica discovery already takes into account any constraints such as finding the primary replica in case of a primary copy approach or finding a replica that can handle additional load. In the second case, information about available replicas can be maintained dynamically by piggybacking it on replies to the client.

Outstanding requests.   The client driver might have submitted a request to the failed replica for which it has not received a reply or where the reply was the failure exception. In this case, the driver has to resubmit the request to the new replica it connects to. In order to guarantee that each request is processed exactly once, each request has to be uniquely identified. This can be achieved by using a counter that is incremented with each new request combined with a unique client identifier. In this way, the server side is able to detect whether the request has already been processed.

When a replica/middleware fails, a client can have an active transaction, i.e., it has already sent read and/or write operations for this transaction, it might have even sent the commit request, but it has not yet received the commit confirmation. Depending on the replica control mechanism outstanding transactions can be resolved in different ways at the server side. They can be simply aborted, they could be committed if the last submitted request was the transaction commit, or they could even be resumed in some protocols if the remaining system has enough information. We present some of them when we discuss the server side failover. The client driver will simply get a reply to its resubmitted request that can be an exception aborting the transaction, the acknowledgement of the commit or the reply to its request.

9.1.4   FAILOVER: SERVER SIDE

At failover time, the server side has to perform several tasks. First, the failure of a replica has to be detected, and all available replicas have to agree on such failure. Second, in the case of a primary copy approach, a new primary has to be selected. Third, atomicity for all outstanding update transactions has to be guaranteed. In particular, for any update transaction that was submitted to the failed replica, either all available replicas commit or abort this transaction. Last, as discussed above, the replicated system must have a means to let the client software know the outcome of a transaction.

Failure detection.   Reliable failure detection is a challenging task because it is difficult to determine whether a process has really failed, is only slow or network connectivity is temporarily interrupted. In this book, we do not discuss the intriguing challenges of failure detection. Instead, we rely on the properties of group communication systems, as discussed in Chapter 4, that include a failure detection mechanism and membership service. Whenever the system detects the failure of a process, it removes the process from the current view of available members and informs the available members delivering the new view. In our case, the members are the replicas. The group communication system usually uses a consensus protocol in order to find agreement on a new view.

Choosing a new primary.   In the case of primary-copy replica control or if a replicated centralized middleware is used with several backups, the failure of the primary/middleware requires to choose a new primary replica/middleware. When failure detection is left to a group communication system, all available replicas will receive the information about the failure as a view change. When a primary fails, one of the available replicas has to be elected as new primary. The simplest approach is to have a deterministic function that, applied over the new view, selects a new primary. For instance, an order can be assigned among all replicas at system start-up, and then each replica can deterministically determine the new primary as the first replica available that appears in the new view. Alternatively, a voting mechanism can be used to determine the new primary.

Deciding on outstanding transactions.   Atomicity should be maintained even in the case of failures. In particular, this means that if a transaction committed (respectively aborted) at the failed replica, it should commit (resp. abort) at the available replicas. A transaction that was submitted to the failed replica and active at the time of the failure, should either commit at all available replicas (but only if the execution was completed and the commit request submitted) or at none of them.

In lazy schemes, a transaction might have committed at the failed replica before the failure but the other replicas have not received the writeset yet. 1-copy-atomicity is violated for this transaction as it does not survive the failure. One might want to try to recover this transaction when the failed replica is recovered, but that would be complicated as thousands of transactions might have committed in between. Thus, if lazy schemes are used, the application must be able to live with the possibility that transactions that committed shortly before the crash are lost.

Eager schemes use a mechanism to guarantee 1-copy-atomicity across all replicas. In this book, we have seen two mechanisms how this can be achieved. The first is based on the traditional 2-phase commit (2PC) protocol as discussed in Chapter 3. The problem with 2PC is its costs and the possibility of blocking. This occurs if the final commit to be sent by the crashed replica, acting as coordinator, does not arrive at any or at some of the replicas. Then, these replicas are blocked. Theoretically, blocking can be avoided if at least one available replica has received the commit decision as it can inform the others. However, such termination protocol is usually not implemented in existing 2PC tools. An alternative is 3PC, which is not blocking, but this protocol is typically not implemented in real databases because it is considered too expensive.

In contrast, replica control algorithms that build upon group communication technology to propagate update and commit information to all replicas can use the uniform reliable delivery property of multicast messages to achieve 1-copy-atomicity. Group communication systems are introduced in Chapter 4, and some example protocols based on their primitives are presented in Chapters 6 and 7. The uniform reliable multicast guarantees that whenever a message is delivered at a replica, even if it crashes immediately after the delivery, it will be delivered to all available replicas. In the protocols described in Chapter 6 and 7, when a replica multicasts a writeset, it waits until it is delivered locally, which is a confirmation that it will be delivered to available replicas, too. The only task left is that they all decide on the same outcome that is guaranteed by the replica control algorithm. Details are given in Chapters 6 and 7 when the individual protocols are discussed.

Client / server interaction. We already indicated that the client software, after detecting a failure of the replica/middleware it is connected to, resubmits the last outstanding request. We have now a closer look at how the server system responds for the protocols we have presented in Chapters 6 and 7. For the centralized protocols, we assume that they follow a centralized replicated approach where there is, in fact, a backup middleware to which the clients reconnect.

We discuss two main cases. In case (i), the client has sent some read and write operations on behalf of a transaction but not yet the commit request when the failure occurs. In case (ii), the client has sent the commit request but the middleware/replica fails before it returns the commit confirmation to the client. In both cases, the client resubmits the last request to the new middleware/replica it connects to.

Let us first look at the pessimistic protocols of Chapter 6. For the centralized middleware approach of Section 6.1, when this middleware fails, all database replicas lose their connections to this middleware. Any active transaction for which the database has not yet received the commit/abort request will be aborted by the database replica. Thus, for transactions for which no commit request was submitted (case (i)), the simplest is to consider them aborted. When the client resubmits its last operation to the new middleware, the middleware simply returns an abort notification. If the client submits the commit request (case (ii)), the new middleware needs to know whether the replicas received the commit request from the failed middleware before the crash or not. This can be achieved by using a 2PC protocol among all replicas, and the middleware backups are also participants in the protocol. Then, the backup middleware will be able to terminate the 2PC protocol as new coordinator.

In the decentralized approaches of Sections 6.2 and 6.3, there are no individual read and write operations, but the entire transaction request is sent in one message. For any transaction request submitted to a replica before it fails, it is either delivered to all replicas or none because of the uniform reliable multicast. Therefore, either all or none execute the transaction. Thus, if the client software resubmits an outstanding transaction request to a new replica after reconnection, the new replica handles it as a new request if the original request was not delivered (multicasting it to all replicas and executing the transaction), or it returns the outcome of the transaction if the original request was delivered.

In Chapter 7, if the centralized middleware in the protocols of Sections 7.2 and 7.3 fails, the database replicas loose their connection to the middleware triggering the abort of any transaction for which they have not yet received the commit request. Thus, the client needs to be informed about this abort when it resubmits its last operation in case (i) above. For case (ii), in the primary copy approach of Section 7.2, the primary could have committed the transaction before the crash or not. If it has, also some of the secondaries could have committed it. The new middleware must know about this. One possibility is to add a write operation to the transaction that inserts the transaction identifier into the database. Then, the new middleware can look for the identifier in each of the database replicas. If it is there, the transaction committed at this replica, if not, it did not commit. If it did not commit at the primary, it has to return an abort to the client. If it committed at the primary but not at some of the secondaries, it can return an ok to the client, and it has to apply the writeset at the secondaries that still miss it. Similarly, in the centralized update anywhere approach of Section 7.3, the backup middleware must know the outcome of the validation, and if positive, must know at which replicas the writeset was already applied. It must respond accordingly to the client and finalize writeset processing. Adding the insert of the transaction identifier as an additional write operation can again help in performing this task.

The distributed approach in Section 7.4 is simpler to handle. The available replicas do not even know about a transaction for which the commit operation was not yet submitted. Thus, when they receive the resubmit of a read or write operation in case (i), they can simply return with an abort information. In case (ii), the writeset was either delivered to all or none of the available replicas. Thus, when the client software resubmits the commit request to a new replica, this replica can respond with the proper outcome if the writeset was delivered or with an abort information if it was not delivered.

9.1.5   RECOVERY

Recovery has the task to restart a failed replica and integrate it into the replicated system. Furthermore, if availability should be increased for a running system, also completely new replicas, that do not yet have any database state, must be integrated into the system. There are several issues to consider. First, as in a non-replicated system, the recovering replica has to bring its own database copy into a consistent state, assuring that the changes of transactions that committed before the crash are integrated in its database image, and no changes of aborted transactions or transactions that were active at the time of the crash are reflected. This *local recovery procedure* is shortly explained in Appendix A.

In a second step, the *data transfer* has to provide the recovering replica with the current state of the database. During its downtime, the remaining system can have committed many transactions, whose changes have to be applied at the recovering replica before it can start processing transactions on its own. If the replica is new, it first has to receive a full database copy.

The final aspect is the coordination with ongoing transaction processing. The simplest method queues any incoming new transactions and waits until all current transactions have terminated. Then, it performs the state transfer, and only once it is completed, transaction processing can resume. As data transfer times can be really large, this would interrupt service for an unacceptable long time resulting in unavailability of the database during recovery. Instead, transaction processing should continue during the data transfer. However, this requires recovery to be synchronized with the execution of transactions. A *recovery coordination* protocol has to guarantee that the recovering replica does not miss the updates of any of transactions that commit during the recovery process. That is, the recovering replica either receives the updates of such a transaction as part of the data transfer or the transaction is handled after the data transfer completed using the standard replica control mechanism in place. The recovery coordination must be specifically designed for the replica control mechanism in place.

In the following, we have a closer look at data transfer recovery coordination.

Data transfer strategies.   There are two main approaches current replication solutions use for data transfer. In both cases, one or more of the available replicas or the middleware are responsible to transfer the data to the recovering replica. The first alternative transfers the entire database state. Such mechanism can, e.g., exploit the load and dump or migration mechanisms that most database systems provide. This mechanism is always needed if a completely new replica is added to the system. In the second alternative, the recovering replica receives and applies all the writesets of transactions that have committed during the replica's downtime. Kernel based replication solutions can directly exploit the standard database log that is also used for local recovery. Middleware based solutions can either resort to log mining facilities, if available, or log the writesets at the middleware level for recovery purposes.

Both alternatives have their drawbacks. A complete database transfer also transfers data items that have not been updated during the recovering replica's downtime. That transfer is unnecessary. Using the writeset transfer, for data items that are frequently updated many updates will be applied during recovery although only the final value is of importance. A general guideline is that the smaller the database and the more transactions the failed replica has missed during its downtime, the more suitable is a full database transfer. However, if the replica was only down for a short time, transferring the writesets is probably more suitable.

In general, the recovering replica only needs the final values of all data items that changed during its downtime. Determining this set, however, is not trivial. It could, e.g., be determined by scanning the writesets and then only apply the latest change for each affected data item. This writeset analysis can be done by the replica that transfers the writesets or by the recovering replica when it receives the writesets. Many different optimizations are possible. However, we are not aware of any system applying them.

Recovery coordination protocol.   While state transfer takes place, transaction processing needs to continue in the rest of the system. The replicas that provide the recovering replica with the data might not be able to execute transactions, at least not at full capacity, but the available replicas that are not involved in the transfer should be able to dedicate their full capacity to transaction processing. The challenge is to guarantee that the recovering replica does not miss any of these transactions. What is needed is basically a *synchronizaton point*. The updates of transactions that committed before the synchronization point are reflected in the data transferred during recovery. At the time of the synchronization point, the recovering replica becomes an available replica, and it applies updates through the standard replica control protocol in place. Finding such a synchronization point is relatively easy in systems with a central middleware or in systems that use a group communication system to multicast writesets to all replicas. In the latter case, once data transfer is nearly completed, the recovering replica can join the replication group and a view change message is delivered at all replicas. This view change message can be used to determines the synchronization point. The updates of transactions delivered before the view change are included in the data transfer; the transactions delivered after the view change are directly processed by the recovering replica.

9.2   SELF-OPTIMIZATION

A system is self-optimizing if it optimally exploits the given resources. The number of replicas is clearly a critical factor. We discuss this in the next section. In this section, we explore optimization possibilities when a fixed number of replicas is provided. A main issue is load-balancing: distributing the incoming requests over all available replicas. Most of this section is dedicated to load-balancing, but we also shortly discuss other measures.

9.2.1   LOAD-BALANCING

The task of load-balancing is to decide where incoming transactions are going to be executed. Clearly, this depends to some extent on the replica control algorithms. But at least read-only transactions can be executed on any replica, independently of the replica control algorithm. When clients connect directly to replicas, they typically submit all their transactions to this local replica. Thus, the only time point for load-balancing is at connection time. In contrast, with a central middleware, all requests are redirected through the middleware, which allows load-balancing on a transaction basis or even an operation basis. In the following, we assume load-balancing is done on a transaction basis.

Load-balancing can provide *load awareness* and *application awareness*. Load-aware load-balancing takes the load on the different replicas into account when assigning transactions to a replica; *application-aware* load-balancing is aware of the access patterns of various transaction types and assigns transactions to replicas so that to exploit commonalities. We have a closer look at some of these strategies.

Load- and application-blind techniques.   The most common and frequently deployed load-balancing strategies are neither load- nor application-aware. But they are simple to implement.

- *Random* simply assigns a transaction randomly to one of the available replicas. Over time, transactions will be equally distributed among the replicas. The advantage of random is that, except of a random number generation module, it requires absolutely no state information.

- *Round-robin* distributes transactions to replicas one by one so that each replica receives exactly the same amount of transactions. This technique requires a minimum amount of state information as the load-balancer has to know, which is the next replica to assign a request to.

Load-aware techniques.   Load-aware techniques take into account that requests can generate different load. If the transaction workload is a mix of simple and complex transactions, then one replica might be easily able to handle two simple transactions concurrently while a single complex transaction might already bring the replica close to saturation. Furthermore, the nodes might have different capacity, and it makes sense to assign them transactions according to their capacity, which means a new transaction should be assigned to a replica that still has the available capacity to execute it. Load-aware techniques are implemented in many domains, not only database replication.

- *Shortest Queue First* considers the number of transactions that are currently executing on a replica and assigns a new transaction to the replica with the fewest number of active transactions. Thus, this technique does not require a lot of information. In particular, it does not require any knowledge about the transactions themselves. However, the number of transactions might not be an exact reflection of the load, as a single complex transaction might require more resources than several simple ones. Nevertheless, it avoids a heavily loaded replica to get more and more transactions that it would not be able to handle.

- *Least Loaded* collects a more accurate picture of the load on each replica. For that, each replica has to provide information about its current load to the load-balancer. This could be CPU and I/O usage. Different to what the title indicates, the load-balancer does not always choose the least loaded replica as the available load information might be somewhat stale. Instead, it ranks replicas according to their load and simply assigns transactions to the less loaded replicas with a higher probability than to the higher loaded replicas. Replicas that are close to saturation will be completely avoided. This mechanism requires the replicas to provide the load-balancer with status information on a regular basis, adding significantly to the complexity.

Application-aware techniques.   If the load-balancer exploits knowledge about the application, it is application-aware.

- *Shortest Execution Length* needs to have an estimate of the execution time of each type of transaction. Typically, the application has a predefined set of transaction types, and, run in isolation, each transaction type has a certain execution time: complex transaction types can take several seconds or even minutes, while simple transaction types can be as short as a few milliseconds. These average execution times can be determined offline and provided to the load-balancer. Then, the load-balancer keeps track of the outstanding transactions at each replica and sums up their estimated execution times. This represents the application-dependent load on this replica. A new transaction is assigned to the replica with the lowest application-dependent load. This mechanism requires a-priori test runs. If execution time for a particular transaction type can vary a lot, then the method is not very precise. It also does not consider that concurrently running transactions can interfere with each other leading to execution times that are very different from those that were measured when transactions run in isolation.

- *Locality-aware request distribution (LARD)* considers the data access patterns of transactions. One of the most expensive costs of transaction execution is secondary storage access when a data item has to be read from disk because it is not yet cached in the database buffer. Often, transactions of the same transaction type access the same tables or data objects. Thus, if transactions of the same type are always sent to the same replica, it is more likely that they find the data they access already in the main memory buffer avoiding expensive I/O. One can even bundle several transaction types into a workload group if they have a large set of overlapping tables. Then, the load-balancer keeps track of where it sends transactions, and when a new transaction comes in, it assigns it to a replica that has executed transactions of the same workload group in the recent past. The idea is that transactions that access the same data are executed by the same replica, allowing the replica to keep all necessary data in main memory. Transactions with different access patterns are distributed across the replicas, so each replica buffers different parts of the database. If there is one dominant transaction type, the replica that is in charge of this transaction type might quickly be overloaded even if it is able to cache all relevant data. Therefore, the approach should be combined with some load-awareness, and assign several replicas to popular transaction types, respectively, workload groups.

  A drawback of this approach is that it might be hard to know the data items that a transaction is going to access. By parsing the application code, it might be easy to determine the database tables, but this is only a rough estimate and might not say a lot about the particular records to be accessed. If the estimates are wrong, LARD might not work as expected.

- *Memory-aware distribution.* LARD does not work if the data set of a workload group does not fit into the main-memory buffer. Then, new data items continuously replace less recently used data. Therefore, memory-aware distribution also takes the size of the data into account and limits a working group to transactions whose combined set fits into main memory.

- *Affinity-based distribution.* Depending on query execution strategies within the database engine, two transactions might not benefit if they run concurrently on the same machine even if they access the same data. For example, when a query requires a simple scan over a relation, the database system often does not use the standard buffer for pages read during the scan. Thus, two transactions that perform a scan over the same relation will both produce I/O, resulting even in a negative effect. Thus, affinity-based balancing only collocates transactions where the common data access actually benefits both, i.e., if their concurrent execution is significantly faster than their sequential execution.

- *Conflict-aware distribution.* In many replica control algorithms, transactions that execute concurrently on one replica are isolated by the concurrency control mechanism of the local database while conflicts between transactions executing on different replicas are often only detected at end of transaction. Thus, if conflicting transactions execute on different replicas, their conflicts are detected very late leading to late aborts. Executing conflicting transactions at the same replica avoids such late abort. Thus, conflict-aware distribution attempts to assign conflicting transactions to the same replica to localize conflicts.

  Determining which transactions conflict in advance is similar to determining the data items they access, and wrong estimates are easily possible.

- *Staleness aware distribution.* Chapter 8 presents lazy protocols that limit the staleness of secondary copies. Some approaches allow each query to indicate its own limit of how much staleness they accept. When such a query is received by the middleware, the middleware has to find a replica that has at most the staleness limit indicated by the query. If no such replica exists, one of the replicas has to be updated to reflect the required staleness level. A load-balancer that considers not only the staleness level, but also the costs associated with bringing a too stale replica up-to-date, is a staleness-aware load-balancer.

Which of the many load-balancing strategies works best strongly depends on the workload, the particular configuration in terms of number of replicas and replica control algorithm, and the overall load submitted to the system. Clearly, simple methods such as random and round-robin are quickly outperformed by more sophisticated techniques. However, the more complex a technique is, the more resources it might need during runtime and more complex techniques are not always better. For example, LARD has shown to work worse than shortest execution length, although on paper it appears appealing. Application-aware mechanisms require a careful analysis of the application beforehand, which might not always be possible. Also, if the application changes, the load-balancer needs to be redesigned.

9.2.2   OTHER OPTIMIZATION TECHNIQUES

Load-balancing is not the only technique that attempts to optimally use the available resources. We briefly discuss two other mechanisms: data placement and load control.

Data placement.   Under partial replication, each data item has only copies on a subset of nodes. The challenge is to decide on the number of copies for each data item and their location. In cluster configurations, where all nodes reside in the same local area network the main goal is typically to keep the update overhead low while providing enough resources to read operations. Thus, the more a data item is updated, the less copies it should have, while the more it is read, the more copies it should have. The system has to find the right replication degree for each data item and distribute the data copies across the nodes such as to have equal load on all nodes.

In contrast, in a wide area setting, data placement is driven by response times. If a data item is not locally available, a remote access is needed. This is expensive if nodes a geographically distributed and connected through the Internet. Furthermore, if a node becomes disconnected from the rest of the system, data items without local copies become unavailable. In this setting, the system has to decide on a data placement that presents a trade-off between avoiding remote access and keeping the global update overhead small. Such data placement should ideally be automatically and dynamically adjusted if the workload changes. Local copies should be created if the fraction of local accesses is high, and be dropped in case there are only few accesses.

Finally, if distributed transactions are to be avoided, data copies have to collocated such that each transaction has a node that has copies of all data items the transaction accesses.

Load control.   Standard optimization techniques, that can already be used in non-replicated systems, are also applicable in replicated environments. For example, load control techniques limit the number of transactions that can be concurrently executed by a single database system, the so-called multi-programming level (MPL). If more transactions are submitted, they are simply queued until running ones complete. Such a limit on the MPL avoids that performance deteriorates when too many requests compete for the same resources. However, the optimal MPL changes with the workload, what means that a dynamic adaptation is required. In a replicated system, MPL limits and load-balancing work together. Load-balancing ensures an even load at global level, while execution at each replica is optimized through local load control.

9.3   ELASTICITY: SELF-PROVISIONING

In this section, we look into elasticity. A system is elastic if it automatically adjusts the number of replicas to the current workload. Elasticity is attained by means of self-provisioning. Self-provisioning adds new replicas to the system if the current system cannot handle the workload anymore and removes unneeded replicas. Self-provisioning has many commonalities with self-healing, but reconfigurations are triggered differently. Self-healing reconfigures the system when failures occur and replicas restart, while self-provisioning reconfigures the system if changes in the global load occur.

9.3.1   SYSTEM RECONFIGURATION

We discussed load-balancing in the previous section as a mechanism to maximize the utilization of available resources. It guarantees an even load across replicas. However, if the load increases, the available computational capacity of the replicated system might not suffice to process the load. This is when self-provisioning comes into place. The self-provisioner determines when reconfiguration is needed and performs the necessary steps to do so. For that, it has to monitor the load on each replica. Simple load imbalances should be handled by the load-balancing component. But if load reaches a threshold on most replicas, e.g., the average replica CPU utilization is above 90%, the addition of a new replica needs to be triggered. If the current workload can be satisfied with a lower number of replicas than currently active, replicas can be removed.

Self-provisioning can be reactive or proactive. A reactive approach triggers a reconfiguration when the load threshold is reached. A proactive approach uses prediction mechanisms in order to perform reconfiguration ahead of time, such that it is completed before saturation occurs. Prediction mechanisms could be based on time series or machine learning approaches.

Removing a replica in case of underload is a fairly simple process. The self-provisioner moves the load of the replica to be decommissioned to the rest of the replicas. In a simple scheme, one can wait until all outstanding transactions have committed while no new transactions are assigned to this replica. Once the replica to be decommissioned does not receive any load, it can be released.

Adding a new replica is conceptually the same as recovering a new replica. First, the entire database copy must be transferred to the new replica. Then it has to receive all updates that occurred during this transfer. This can be a lengthy process. The problem can be alleviated by keeping two sets of replicas. The active replicas execute transactions. Inactive replicas do not get any transactions assigned, i.e., they do not have any local transactions. Furthermore, their database copies get updated in a lazy fashion either by sending them the writesets or by providing them with periodic checkpoints. In this way, adding one of the inactive replicas to the set of active replicas takes similar time or is even faster than recovering a failed replica that was down for a short time. However, the approach consumes resources on replicas that are inactive as they have to install writesets or checkpoints on a regular basis.

9.3.2   DECIDING ON THE RIGHT NUMBER OF REPLICAS

Load metric.   One of the most critical factors for self-provisioning is the metric to be used for measuring the replica load. One possibility is to measure the *resources* used by each replica such as *CPU* and *disk utilization*. One of the main difficulties is that bottlenecks move from one resource to another when the workload varies. For instance, if the workload consists of a high percentage of complex read operations and most of the data reside in the database cache, then the CPU becomes the bottleneck. In contrast, update intensive workloads requiring many disk writes and read-only workloads scanning large parts of the database that do not fit into main memory, are I/O bound as the disk becomes the bottleneck. The load metric needs to be complete enough to determine the type of workload that triggered the bottleneck. For instance, adding new replicas does not help update intensive workloads if the number of replicas has reached the scalability limit. In contrast, read-intensive workloads can always be scaled by adding new replicas.

A different type of metric is response time. Often, service providers offer service level agreements that guarantee a certain performance. For instance, the service level agreement could specify that most of the transactions (e.g., 90% of all transactions) must complete within a certain response time limit (e.g., two seconds). In this case, self-provisioning is triggered to add more replicas once more than the agreed percentage of transactions takes longer than the specified limit. Average response time can be an alternative metric.

Cost prediction.   The provisioning process itself takes time and resources. Especially, adding a new replica is cost- and time-consuming. Depending on whether a completely new replica is added, or an inactive replica that already has a stale version of the database, reconfiguration times can vary significantly. They are determined by the size of the database, and the number of writesets to be transferred and applied. The costs and time of these processes can be estimated by running extensive offline tests for different database sizes and number of writesets to be transferred.

Proactive provisioning can help in starting reconfiguration ahead of time so that the new replica is available when the workload has reached the level at which a new replica is necessary.

Monitoring.   Monitoring the load has also a cost attached to it. The more data are collected the more does monitoring have an impact on the performance of the system. The right tradeoff has to be found. Furthermore, the monitoring component also needs to take into account other activities that execute in the underlying system. For instance, many database systems perform periodic tasks such as checkpoints, compressing pages, etc. that consume resources temporarily but have nothing to do with the current workload. Finally, while reconfiguration takes place, monitoring should be interrupted because system performance will deviate from its typical behavior.

9.4   RELATED WORK

Self-healing.   Most replication approaches include failure handling, and we have discussed the related literature throughout the book. Thus, here we mainly focus on recovery. First recovery procedures for a kernel based replicated system are presented by Kemme et al. [2001]. Several data transfer strategies and their synchronization with ongoing transaction processing are presented. Jiménez-Peris et al. [2002a] present a middleware based recovery protocol where the middleware logs writesets and uses multiple recoverers to transfer state concurrently. Liang and Kemme [2008] provide an evaluation of recovery protocols that determines, depending on database size and the number and size of writesets, which of two strategies is more efficient. Vilaça et al. [2009] study the impact of having multiple recoverers and flow control. Recovery for warehouses distributed over the Internet has been proposed by Lau and Madden [2006], and recovery for main-memory database replication is discussed by Manassiev and Amza [2007].

In a different context, Vandiver et al. [2007] introduce a Byzantine replication database protocol to tolerate intrusions in databases. They discuss how to integrate the Byzantine agreement with the replica control of the database. Preguiça et al. [2008] exploit snapshot isolation in the context of Byzantine fault tolerance. Gashi et al. [2007] present a replication approach that tolerates software faults in database engines. By having diverse databases, they are able to mask software faults, for instance, in SQL processing, or faults that make a database engine crash. Diverse database replication has some commonalities to Byzantine replication but focuses on tolerating design failures instead of intrusions. Byzantine fault tolerance implies to have some kind of Byzantine agreement that is typically very expensive, while diverse database replication has similar cost as regular database replication. Interestingly, the only architectural choice for diverse database replication is a middleware based approach in order to support the heterogeneity of database engines.

Self-optimization.   Load-balancing is a well-explored research area. From the techniques presented in Section 9.2, shortest execution length and locality-aware request distribution are proposed by Amza et al. [2005], memory-aware distribution by Elnikety et al. [2007], affinity-based distribution by Röhm et al. [2000], conflict-aware distribution by Zuikeviciute and Pedone [2008], and staleness aware distribution by Röhm et al. [2002] and Gançarski et al. [2007]. Load-balancing for pessimistic replica control with decentralized middlewares is presented by Milán et al. [2004]. The challenge is to distribute transaction execution equally across all replicas while clients are connected to one of the many replicas. The paper also combines load-balancing with limiting the MPL [Heiss and Wagner, 1991] locally at each replica. External control over MPLs is proposed by Schroeder et al. [2006]. In the context of partial replication, Wolfson et al. [1997] consider data placement taking into account the read and write load on each data item, while Serrano et al. [2008] perform adaptation of the number of data copies in a wide area setting adding copies to nodes when local clients request them, and removing them if they are not needed.

Self-provisioning.   Self-provisioning of replicated database systems has been first described by Soundararajan and Amza [2006] proposing a reactive provisioning approach for a fully replicated system. Chen et al. [2006] improve over the previous approach by using a proactive approach based on offline learning which predicts for a particular application when the load increases. Thus, provisioning new replicas can be done earlier than in a reactive approach. Soundararajan et al. [2006] study self-provisioning in the context of multiple applications sharing the same database. Adding data copies dynamically to nodes in partially replicated systems can also be considered a form of self-provisioning [Serrano et al., 2008; Wolfson et al., 1997].

CHAPTER 10

Other Aspects of Replication

In this last chapter, we discuss shortly other aspects of database replication.

- Database systems typically represent the backend tier of multi-tier information systems and other tiers might cache data from the database tier for faster access. This requires replica control across tiers. We discuss multi-tier architectures in Section 10.1.

- Quorum systems are an alternative to ROWA where both read and write operations only access a quorum of replicas, guaranteeing that conflicts become visible at least one replica. They are discussed in Section 10.2.

- In this book, we have focused on traditional distributed database systems, where we can expect to scale to tens or at most hundreds of nodes, and we assume standard wide and local area communication. Section 10.3 provides an outlook at the challenges associated with data replication in other computing environment such as mobile computing with very limited and unreliable connectivity, and peer-to-peer systems that might scale up to thousands of nodes.

10.1 MULTI-TIER ARCHITECTURES

Modern information systems usually follow a multi-tier architecture. The client is a web-browser or uses an API based on web-services. Client requests are received by a web server which implements the presentation logic providing static content and web-page generation. More complex requests are forwarded to the application server, which implements the application logic. The application server calls the backend database tier when business critical data are accessed as such data are maintained by a database server. In most cases, the web-server is stateless, meaning that no state is maintained between client requests. However, the application server often caches data from the persistent tier, often in object-oriented format, as this is the prevalent data model for application programming. In principle, a cached data item is a replicated data item that only exists for limited time. Thus, cache consistency protocols are required that have some similarities with replica control algorithms. Furthermore, application servers are often replicated by themselves, leading to further replication of the database items.

In a typical execution, whenever an application program requires a database item for the first time, it first checks whether the data item already resides in the local cache. If yes, the cached copy is used. Only if the data item is not in the cache, a query to the database system is issued, the data item retrieved, transformed into the object-oriented model, and stored in the cache. As several programs might access the cache concurrently, the cache has to implement some concurrency control protocol.

Current application server technology uses the cache often only if requests are for individual data items, identified by their primary key, as the application server and its cache usually lack query functionality. Declarative queries with search predicates are therefore sent directly to the database system ignoring any data items that might be cached. This execution has similarities with a replicated system where some requests are directed to the cache and others to the database. Interestingly, if the cache uses a locking-based concurrency control and the underlying database uses snapshot isolation, execution can easily be neither 1-copy-serializable nor provide 1-copy-snapshot isolation [Perez-Sorrosal et al., 2007].

Things can become even more complicated if the application server is replicated and each server instance has its own database cache. Then, when one application server updates a data item, its copy in the cache will be updated but not the others. Most systems use cache invalidation schemes to notify other caches that their copies have become invalid. If transactions at these remote instances have already accessed some data items, they must be aborted. Invalidation is usually done lazily, after transaction commit. Therefore, similar conflict problems as with lazy update anywhere can therefore occur.

10.2   QUORUMS

ROWA approaches require all replicas to be available to execute a write operation while ROWAA protocols require complex failover mechanisms to detect failures and exclude the failed replica in a proper way. Quorums systems avoid these problems and achieve availability in a simple way. The idea is that each write operation only accesses a quorum of replicas. A quorum must include enough replicas to guarantee that each two write operations access at least one common replica. Then, conflicts can be detected and serialized at this replica. A typical quorum could be the majority of replicas, i.e., $n/2 + 1$ in an n-node system. Using quorums there is no need for failure detection and failover. Each write request must simply find a quorum of available replicas to succeed. Recovery is also very simple. When a failed replica rejoins the system, the first write that chooses the replica to be included in its quorum writes the data copy of this replica, which becomes current.

Writing only a quorum of replicas makes read operations more complex. It is not enough that they read any copy if they want to have the guarantee to read the latest version. Instead, they also have to read a quorum of replicas so that any read quorum overlaps with every possible write quorum. Then, it is guaranteed that one of the copies that they access will have the latest value. In order to determine which of them has actually the latest value, write operations need to timestamp the data copies in order to create one total order of updates on any given data item.

Despite their elegance, quorums have never been used in any commercial database system. One of the reasons might be the need for timestamps for each data items, which is difficult to achieve in a relational database system. However, the main reason is likely the increased costs for read operations [Jiménez-Peris et al., 2003]. In basically all applications, read operations are much more frequent than write operations, and the performance penalty is simply too high.

However, with the rapid development of data centers, large scale data management and cloud computing, quorum systems have suddenly received unprecedented attention. The main focus lies on availability. As large scale systems increasingly start to rely on commodity hardware as storage resources, not only single failures but concurrent failures have become common. For such storage systems, quorum systems appear attractive to efficiently write data to stable storage in a reliable manner. First large scale implementations have been conducted [Chandra et al., 2007], and quorum libraries start to be available. Nevertheless, building quorum systems remains highly complex.

10.3   MOBILE AND PEER-TO-PEER ENVIRONMENTS

This book has focused on traditional database replication in local- and wide area networks, considering scalability in the tens or at most hundreds of replicas. However, data replication is also crucial in other domains such as mobile and peer-to-peer environments.

Mobile environments.   There are several fundamental differences between a mobile environment and the wired world. First, communication is slow and unreliable, bandwidth is low, and disconnections occur frequently. Secondly, the capacity of mobile devices ranges from powerful laptops to tiny sensors with considerable less computing power and memory. Replication in such environments is used for availability during periods of disconnection, and for fast local access. Synchronization and replica control will likely occur always in a lazy fashion. Replicated data management in mobile environments is discussed in detail by Terry [2008].

Peer-to-peer environments.   In peer-to-peer environments, each node is server and client at the same time, providing service and content to others while requesting them from other nodes. Peer-to-peer systems can scale to hundreds of thousands of nodes. They are organized in application-level overlays, sometimes structured, sometimes only loosely connected. One of the main applications of peer-to-peer systems is file sharing. People download files from others and offer their files to the community. With every download, a new copy of a file is automatically created.

The tasks and challenges related to data replication in such environments are fundamentally different to traditional database replication. One major challenge is search, that is, to find peers that have copies of the requested data items. A second issue is to efficiently download files and truly share the load among all peers. A third challenge is to maintain the overlay structure despite frequent failures, disconnects and newly arriving peers. Data consistency, in contrast, plays only a minor role. Most data items are believed to change seldom. In any case, transactional properties are rarely considered, and achieving eventual consistency is already a challenging goal given the scale and dynamics of such systems.

APPENDIX A

Transactions and the ACID Properties

A database can be seen as a set of data items $x, y, \ldots$. An application encapsulates its data accesses into logical units called transactions. A transaction T_i is a sequence of read operations $r_i(x)$ and write operations $w_i(x)$ on data items. A database system provides certain properties when executing transactions, referred to as the ACID properties: atomicity, consistency, isolation and durability.

A.1 ATOMICITY

Atomicity reflects the all-or-nothing property. A transaction T_i either executes completely and terminates with a commit operation (indicated as c_i), or it aborts (indicated as a_i), in which case, it should not leave any effect in the database. An abort can be induced due to several reasons. For example, the application program can decide on abort due to application semantics (e.g., there is not enough money in the account to perform a withdraw), or there is some failure (the connection between client and database system is broken). If a transaction has already executed some write operation $w_i(x)$ and then aborts, the changes it performed on x need to be undone. This process is called *local undo recovery*. There are several mechanisms to achieve is. For example, before $w_i(x)$ is executed, the *before-image* of x can be logged. When an abort occurs, a compensation operation $w_i^{-1}(x)$ sets x back to the value of the before-image. Alternatively, the write operation $w_i(x)$ might actually not change x but perform the operation on a temporary copy of x. At the time of an abort, this temporary copy is simply discarded. Only if the transaction commits, the value of the temporary copy is applied to x.

A.2 CONSISTENCY

Assuming the database is in a consistent state before a transaction starts, consistency guarantees that the database is again in a consistent state when the transaction commits. This is a quite fuzzy property. Consistency depends on the application semantics and application programmers are responsible to define the individual read and write operations of transactions. If the operations generate inconsistency, then the database has no means to know that. However, database systems provide mechanisms to help database designers to specify integrity constraints, which are constraints that should hold over any instance of the database. For instance, the application might require every client to receive a unique identifier, every bill to refer to an existing client, and every account to have a non-negative balance. The first constrained can be achieved by defining an attribute in the client table to be a primary key. The database will then disallow two tuples to have the same value in the primary key. The second constrained can be specified through a foreign key which requires each bill tuple to point to a client tuple. The third constrained can be achieved by restricting the domain of the balance attribute. In summary, database systems provide an interface to define common constraints at design time and enforce these constraints during runtime.

A.3   DURABILITY

Durability guarantees that committed transactions are not lost despite failures. The typical failure types considered are process failure (the process(es) running the database management systems crash) or the machine on which the database management system runs, crashes, e.g., because of a power outage. In general, it is assumed that all information in main memory is lost or corrupted, but all information that was written to stable storage, typically a disk system, remains accessible. Thus, before a transaction commits, enough information must be made persistent so that all changes performed by the transaction are reflected on stable storage. In the simplest case, all disk pages changed by a transaction are written to disk before commit. However, as random access to stable storage is expensive, many database systems only write the after-images of changed records to an append-only log. Only the log is flushed to disk whenever a transaction commits making transaction execution faster. However, when a database recovers after a crash, committed transactions whose changes are not reflected on the database pages on disk have to be redone. This is done by scanning the log and installing the corresponding after-images.

   In the case of a crash, atomicity also needs to be revisited. When a transaction is active at the time of a crash it is impossible for the system to guarantee successful completion. However, it might be possible that some changes were already written to stable storage before the crash. At the time of recovery, these changes have to be undone, just as it is necessary to undo changes when a transaction aborts during normal processing. Therefore, before-images are typically also appended to the log, and the log is flushed before a data page is written to disk. At the time of recovery after a failure, these before-images might need to be installed for active or aborted transactions depending on the state on the data pages.

A.4   ISOLATION

If all transactions only read data items, then running them concurrently is no problem. However, as soon as updates occur, problems arise and the database system has to properly isolate transactions. In the ideal world, the concurrent execution of a set of transactions should be equivalent to a serial execution of these transactions. That is, if there are two transactions T_i and T_j and their execution interleaves (e.g., they execute their operations in alternating order), it should appear to both transactions as if either T_i completely executed before T_j or T_j executed completely before T_i. That is, each transaction should have the impression it is alone in the system. Such an execution, also

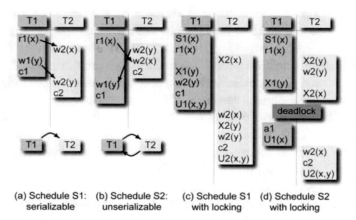

(a) Schedule S1: serializable
(b) Schedule S2: unserializable
(c) Schedule S1 with locking
(d) Schedule S2 with locking

Figure A.1: Example executions

called schedule, is called *serializable*, as it is equivalent to a serial execution. If T_i and T_j access disjoint data sets, then isolation is trivially fulfilled. Any interleaving execution is serializable. However, if they access common data items, isolation is more difficult to achieve. In the case of read operations, there is still no problem as they do not affect each other. However, as soon as there is one write operation on a data item x, and the other transaction has either also a write or a read on x, the operations affect each other; we say they *conflict*. If T_i writes x and T_j reads it, there is a difference whether T_j reads x before or after T_i's write. Similar, if both write x, the order matters as it determines the final value of x.

Figure A.1 shows two examples of interleaved schedules. Time passes from top to bottom. In both schedules, T_1 first reads x and then writes y. In Schedule $S1$, T_2 first writes x and then y. In schedule $S2$, it first rites y and then x. Schedule $S1$ of Figure A.1(a) is serializable, as for both pairs of conflicting operations ($r_1(x)/w_2(x)$ and $w_1(y)/w_2(y)$), T_1's operations executes before T_2's operation. Thus, the schedule is equivalent to an execution where T_1 executes completely before T_2. Schedule $S2$ of Figure A.1(b) is not serializable. $r_1(x)$ executes before $w_2(x)$ but $w_1(y)$ executes after $w_2(y)$. But in a serial execution T_1 before T_2 both of T_1's operations execute before T_2 operations, and in a serial execution T_2 before T_1 it is the other way around. Whether an execution is serializable can be tested using a serialization graph. The transactions are the nodes and there is an edge from transaction T_i to T_j if one of T_i's operations is executed before a conflicting operation of T_j. The serialization graph of the execution of Figure A.1(a), is shown just below the schedule itself, and has only an edge from T_1 to T_2, while the serialization graph of Figure A.1(b) has edges in both directions, and thus, a cycle. In fact, a schedule is serializable if the serialization graph is acyclic [Bernstein et al., 1987].

Concurrency Control   Transaction isolation is enforced by the means of a concurrency control protocol. These protocols can be classified into two different families: pessimistic and optimistic. Pessimistic protocols generally use locking. Before a transaction wants to read a data item x it has to acquire a shared lock on x before a write it has to acquire an exclusive lock. A shared lock is only granted if there are at most other shared locks on a data item. An exclusive lock is only granted if there are no other locks granted on the data item. This allows read operations to execute concurrently on the data item, but only one write operation at a time. If a lock cannot be granted, the requesting transaction is blocked until the conflicting locks are released. In order to provide serializability (and for some other reasons such as proper abort), transactions typically release all their locks only at the end of execution, just after commit or abort. This mechanism is called strict 2-phase locking (strict 2PL). In the first phase, during transaction execution all locks are requested step by step as the operations are executed. At the end of transaction (second phase), all locks are released in one step.

Figure A.1(c) shows how the execution of Figure A.1(a) is changed through locking. When T_1 submits its read operation $r_1(x)$, it first requests are shared lock (denoted as $S1(x)$ in the figure). The lock is granted and T_1 performs the operation. When now T_2 submits $w_2(x)$, it requests an exclusive lock on x (denoted as $X2(x)$ in the figure) but is blocked. As long as the transaction is blocked, it cannot perform any further operations. Thus, the next operation is $w_1(y)$, and T_1 receives an exclusive lock on y. After its commit, both locks are released (denoted as an U for unlock in the figure). Now T_2 gets its lock, executes its write on x, acquires an exclusive lock on y, updates y and finally commits and releases both locks. Figure A.1(d) shows the execution when the submission order is as in Figure A.1(b). T_1 gets a shared lock on x and T_2 an exclusive lock on y. When T_1 now requests an exclusive lock on y it is blocked, and so is T_2 when it requests the exclusive lock on x. A deadlock has occurred. The database system has to detect it. It will abort one of the transactions, which then releases its locks and the other transaction can continue. In the example, T_1 is aborted and T_2 can finish its execution.

Locking might block transactions unnecessarily. In the first example above, the execution would have been serializable, but locking nevertheless blocks T_2 until all of T_1 has completed. In order to achieve more concurrency, optimistic protocols have been proposed. Whenever a transaction accesses a data item, it creates a local copy and performs all write operations on the local copy. At the end of the execution, a transaction checks whether its execution has been serializable. For instance, if the transaction has read a data item x and another transaction has updated x and committed since then, execution could potentially be unserializable. In such a case, a transaction is forced to abort. In a simple form of optimistic concurrency control, the validation phase checks whether the read-set of the transaction, i.e., the set of data items it has read, overlaps with the write-set of any concurrent transaction that already has performed a successful validation. If this is the case, the transaction aborts (simply discarding its local item copies). Otherwise, validation succeeds, and the transaction writes all the items it has changed into the database. This final phase is called the commit phase. At most, one transaction can be in validation or commit phase. Many variations of optimistic concurrency control have been proposed in the past.

A.5   DISTRIBUTED TRANSACTIONS AND 2-PHASE COMMIT

In a distributed database, the data items of the database are distributed among several database nodes. Each data item resides on exactly one node. When a transaction wants to access data items that reside on different node, it turns into a *distributed transaction*. With this, enforcing the ACID properties becomes more challenging. A particular concern is atomicity, namely that if a transaction commits resp. aborts at one of the participating nodes, it has to commit resp. abort at all participating nodes. This is tricky to achieve when there are failures. Therefore, a distributed coordination protocol is needed that guarantees atomicity across all nodes. The best known protocol is 2-phase commit (2PC). We only shortly outline the principles steps of 2PC here and refer the reader to Özsu and Valduriez [1999] for a detailed discussion.

When the transaction wants to commit, one of the nodes becomes the coordinator of the commit processing. It sends a PREPARE-TO-COMMIT message to all participating nodes. When a participating node receives this message and is willing to commit it sends a PREPARED message back to the coordinator. If it wants to abort the transaction, it sends an ABORT message back to the coordinator and aborts the transaction locally. If the coordinator has received PREPARED messages from all participants, it commits the transaction locally and sends a COMMIT message to all participants. Upon receiving such message, a participant commits. If one of the participants has returned an ABORT, the coordinator aborts the transaction and sends an ABORT to all participants that had sent a PREPARED message. They will also abort the transaction. Clearly, this protocol commits a transaction at all nodes if all participants send a PREPARED message and aborts a transaction at all nodes as soon as at least one participant sends an ABORT message. But this is only true of there are no failures.

In order to handle failures, nodes have to write information to their log on stable storage at certain time points. In particular, before the coordinator sends a message (PREPARE-TO-COMMIT, COMMIT, ABORT), it writes in its log that it is sending the message. Before a participating node sends the PREPARED message, it writes enough information into stable storage that it is able to either commit or abort the message. It also writes into the log that it has sent the PRE-PARED message. When a participants aborts or commits a transaction it writes a corresponding COMMIT/ABORT log entry.

Failures can occur any time during the execution of the protocol. If a participant fails before sending a PREPARED or ABORT to the coordinator, the coordinator will time out waiting for the response. At this time, it can simply decide to abort the transaction as it is sure that no node has committed the transaction yet. If the coordinator fails before a participant receives the PREPARE-TO-COMMIT, it can also abort the transaction as the coordinator cannot commit the transaction before receiving the PREPARED messages. However, if the coordinator fails after having sent the PREPARE-TO-COMMIT message but before sending the COMMIT/ABORT message, a participant that had sent the PREPARED message does not know the outcome. It is blocked until the coordinator is recovered.

When the coordinator or a participant recovers after a failure, it will find enough information in stable storage to know the state of the transaction. For instance, if the participant finds out that is has sent the PREPARED message but failed before committing/aborting the transaction, it can ask the coordinator for the final outcome.

Bibliography

A. El Abbadi and S. Toueg. Availability in partitioned replicated databases. In *Proc. 5th ACM SIGACT-SIGMOD Symp. on Principles of Database Systems*, pages 240–251, 1986. DOI: 10.1145/6012.15418 64

A. Adya. *Weak Consistency: A Generalized Theory and Optimistic Implementations for Distributed Transactions*. PhD thesis, Computer Science and Artificial Intelligence Laboratory, MIT, Cambridge, 1999. 70

D. Agrawal, G. Alonso, A. El Abbadi, and I. Stanoi. Exploiting atomic broadcast in replicated databases (extended abstract). In *Proc. 3rd Int. Euro-Par Conf.*, pages 496–503, 1997. DOI: 10.1007/BFb0002775 64

F. Akal, C. Türker, H-J Schek, Y. Breitbart, T. Grabs, and L. Veen. Fine-grained replication and scheduling with freshness and correctness guarantees. In *Proc. 31st Int. Conf. on Very Large Data Bases*, pages 565–576, 2005. 101

R. Alonso, D. Barbará, and H. Garcia-Molina. Data caching issues in an information retrieval system. *ACM Trans. Database Syst.*, 15(3):359–384, 1990. DOI: 10.1145/88636.87848 101

Y. Amir and C. Tutu. From total order to database replication. In *Proc. 22nd Int. Conf. on Distributed Computing Systems*, pages 494–503, 2002. DOI: 10.1109/ICDCS.2002.1022299 45

C. Amza, A. L. Cox, and W. Zwaenepoel. Distributed versioning: Consistent replication for scaling back-end databases of dynamic content web sites. In *Proc. ACM/IFIP/USENIX Int. Middleware Conf.*, pages 282–302, 2003a. 45, 64, 65

C. Amza, A. L. Cox, and W. Zwaenepoel. Conflict-aware scheduling for dynamic content applications. In *Proc. 4th USENIX Symp. on Internet Tech. and Systems*, 2003b. 45, 65

C. Amza, A. L. Cox, and W. Zwaenepoel. A comparative evaluation of transparent scaling techniques for dynamic content servers. In *Proc. 21st Int. Conf. on Data Engineering*, pages 230–241, 2005. DOI: 10.1109/ICDE.2005.6 117

T. A. Anderson, Y. Breitbart, H. F. Korth, and A. Wool. Replication, consistency, and practicality: Are these mutually exclusive? In *Proc. ACM SIGMOD Int. Conf. on Management of Data*, pages 484–495, 1998. DOI: 10.1145/276305.276347 64

H. Berenson, P. Bernstein, J. Gray, J. Melton, E. O'Neil, and P. O'Neil. A critique of ANSI SQL isolation levels. In *Proc. ACM SIGMOD Int. Conf. on Management of Data*, pages 1–10, 1995. DOI: 10.1145/568271.223785 12

J. Bernabé-Gisbert, V. Zuikeviciute, F. D. Muñoz-Escoí, and F. Pedone. A probabilistic analysis of snapshot isolation with partial replication. In *Proc. 27th Symp. on Reliable Distributed Systems*, pages 249–258, 2008. DOI: 10.1109/SRDS.2008.10 46, 52, 87

Ph. A. Bernstein and N. Goodman. An algorithm for concurrency control and recovery in replicated distributed databases. *ACM Trans. Database Syst.*, 9(4):596–615, 1984. DOI: 10.1145/1994.2207 64

Ph. A. Bernstein, V. Hadzilacos, and N. Goodman. *Concurrency Control and Recovery in Database Systems*. Addison-Wesley, 1987. 10, 12, 64, 125

Ph. A. Bernstein, A. Fekete, H. Guo, R. Ramakrishnan, and P. Tamma. Relaxed-currency serializ-ability for middle-tier caching and replication. In *Proc. ACM SIGMOD Int. Conf. on Management of Data*, pages 599–610, 2006. DOI: 10.1145/1142473.1142540 101

K. P. Birman, A. Schiper, and P. Stephenson. Lightweigt causal and atomic group multicast. *ACM Trans. Comp. Syst.*, 9(3):272–314, 1991. DOI: 10.1145/128738.128742 46

Y. Breitbart, R. Komondoor, R. Rastogi, S. Seshadri, and A. Silberschatz. Update propagation protocols for replicated databases. In *Proc. ACM SIGMOD Int. Conf. on Management of Data*, pages 97–108, 1999. DOI: 10.1145/304181.304191 102

M. J. Carey and M. Livny. Conflict detection tradeoffs for replicated data. *ACM Trans. Database Syst.*, 16(4):703–746, 1991. DOI: 10.1145/115302.115289 52, 64

E. Cecchet, J. Marguerite, and W. Zwaenepoel. C-JDBC: Flexible database clustering middleware. In *Proc. USENIX 2004 Annual Technical Conf., FREENIX Track*, pages 9–18, 2004. 45, 64, 65

E. Cecchet, G. Candea, and A. Ailamaki. Middleware-based database replication: the gaps between theory and practice. In *Proc. ACM SIGMOD Int. Conf. on Management of Data*, pages 739–752, 2008. DOI: 10.1145/1376616.1376691 46

T. D. Chandra, R. Griesemer, and J. Redstone. Paxos made live: an engineering perspective. In *Proc. ACM SIGACT-SIGOPS 26th Symp. on the Principles of Distributed Computing*, pages 398–407, 2007. DOI: 10.1145/1281100.1281103 121

J. Chen, G. Soundararajan, and C. Amza. Autonomic provisioning of backend databases in dynamic content web servers. In *Proc. 3rd Int. Conf. on Autonomic Computing*, pages 231–242, 2006. DOI: 10.1109/ICAC.2006.1662403 117

G. Chockler, I. Keidar, and R. Vitenberg. Group communication specifications: a comprehensive study. *ACM Comp. Surv.*, 33(4):427–469, 2001. DOI: 10.1145/503112.503113 46

P. Chundi, D. J. Rosenkrantz, and S. S. Ravi. Deferred updates and data placement in distributed databases. In *Proc. 12th Int. Conf. on Data Engineering*, pages 469–476, 1996. DOI: 10.1109/ICDE.1996.492196 102

A. Correia, J. Pereira, L. Rodrigues, N. Carvalho, R. Vilaça, R. Oliveira, and S. Guedes. Gorda: An open architecture for database replication. In *Proc. IEEE Int. Symp. on Networking Computing and Applications*, pages 287–290, 2007. DOI: 10.1109/NCA.2007.26 45

K. Daudjee and K. Salem. Lazy database replication with ordering guarantees. In *Proc. 20th Int. Conf. on Data Engineering*, pages 424–435, 2004. DOI: 10.1109/ICDE.2004.1320016 15, 101

K. Daudjee and K. Salem. Lazy database replication with snapshot isolation. In *Proc. 32nd Int. Conf. on Very Large Data Bases*, pages 715–726, 2006. 87

S. Elnikety, F. Pedone, and W. Zwaenopoel. Database replication using generalized snapshot isolation. In *Proc. 24th Symp. on Reliable Distributed Systems*, pages 73–84, 2005. DOI: 10.1109/RELDIS.2005.14 87

S. Elnikety, S. G. Dropsho, and F. Pedone. Tashkent: uniting durability with transaction ordering for high-performance scalable database replication. In *Proc. 1st ACM SIGOPS/EuroSys European Conf. on Computer Systems*, pages 117–130, 2006. DOI: 10.1145/1217935.1217947 45, 46, 87

S. Elnikety, S. G. Dropsho, and W. Zwaenepoel. Tashkent+: memory-aware load balancing and update filtering in replicated databases. In *Proc. 2nd ACM SIGOPS/EuroSys European Conf. on Computer Systems*, pages 399–412, 2007. DOI: 10.1145/1272996.1273037 117

S. Elnikety, S. G. Dropsho, E. Cecchet, and W. Zwaenepoel. Predicting replicated database scalability from standalone database profiling. In *Proc. 4th ACM SIGOPS/EuroSys European Conf. on Computer Systems*, pages 303–316, 2009. DOI: 10.1145/1519065.1519098 52

A. Fekete, D. Liarokapis, E. O'Neil, P. O'Neil, and D. Shasha. Making snapshot isolation serializable. *ACM Trans. Database Syst.*, 30(2):492–528, 2005. DOI: 10.1145/1071610.1071615 70

U. Fritzke Jr and Ph. Ingels. Transactions on partially replicated data based on reliable and atomic multicasts. In *Proc. 21st Int. Conf. on Distributed Computing Systems*, pages 284–291, 2001. DOI: 10.1109/ICDSC.2001.918958 46

S. Gançarski, H. Naacke, E. Pacitti, and P. Valduriez. The Leganet system: Freshness-aware transaction routing in a database cluster. *Information Systems*, 32(2):320–343, 2007. DOI: 10.1016/j.is.2005.09.004 101, 117

132   BIBLIOGRAPHY

I. Gashi, P. Popov, and L. Strigini. Fault tolerance via diversity for off-the-shelf products: A study with SQL database servers. *IEEE Trans. Dependable Sec. Comput.*, 4(4):280–294, 2007. DOI: 10.1109/TDSC.2007.70208 116

J. Gray, P. Helland, P. E. O'Neil, and D. Shasha. The dangers of replication and a solution. In *Proc. ACM SIGMOD Int. Conf. on Management of Data*, pages 173–182, 1996. DOI: 10.1145/235968.233330 5, 24, 30, 64

H. Guo, P. Larson, R. Ramakrishnan, and J. Goldstein. Relaxed currency and consistency: How to say "good enough" in SQL. In *Proc. ACM SIGMOD Int. Conf. on Management of Data*, pages 815–826, 2004. DOI: 10.1145/1007568.1007661 101

M. Hayden. The Ensemble system. Technical report, Department of Computer Science, Cornell University, 1998. 46

H-U. Heiss and R. Wagner. Adaptive load control in transaction processing systems. In *Proc. 17th Int. Conf. on Very Large Data Bases*, pages 47–54, 1991. 117

J. Holliday, D. Agrawal, and A. El Abbadi. The performance of database replication with group multicast. In *Proc. of the IEEE Int. Conf. on Fault-Tolerant Computing Systems*, pages 158–165, 1999. DOI: 10.1109/FTCS.1999.781046 64

J. Holliday, D. Agrawal, and A. El Abbadi. Partial database replication using epidemic communication. In *Proc. 22nd Int. Conf. on Distributed Computing Systems*, pages 485–493, 2002. DOI: 10.1109/ICDCS.2002.1022298 46

JGroups. *JGroups: A Toolkit for Reliable Multicast Communication.* http://www.jgroups.org; accessed on August, 4, 2010. 46

R. Jiménez-Peris, M. Patiño-Martínez, and G. Alonso. Non-intrusive, parallel recovery of replicated data. In *Proc. 21st Symp. on Reliable Distributed Systems*, pages 150–159, 2002a. DOI: 10.1109/RELDIS.2002.1180183 116

R. Jiménez-Peris, M. Patiño-Martínez, B. Kemme, and G. Alonso. Improving the scalability of fault-tolerant database clusters. In *Proc. 22nd Int. Conf. on Distributed Computing Systems*, pages 477–484, 2002b. DOI: 10.1109/ICDCS.2002.1022297 45, 50, 64, 65

R. Jiménez-Peris, M. Patiño-Martínez, G. Alonso, and B. Kemme. Are quorums an alternative for data replication? *ACM Trans. Database Syst.*, 28(3):257–294, 2003. DOI: 10.1145/937598.937601 52, 120

B. Kemme. One-copy-serializability. In L. Liu and M. T. Özsu, editors, *Encyclopedia of Database Systems*, pages 1947–1948. Springer US, 2009. DOI: 10.1007/978-0-387-39940-9 12

B. Kemme and G. Alonso. A new approach to developing and implementing eager database replication protocols. *ACM Trans. Database Syst.*, 25(3):333–379, 2000a. DOI: 10.1145/363951.363955 64

B. Kemme and G. Alonso. Don't be lazy, be consistent: Postgres-R, a new way to implement database replication. In *Proc. 26th Int. Conf. on Very Large Data Bases*, pages 134–143, 2000b. 45, 64

B. Kemme, A. Bartoli, and Ö. Babaoglu. Online reconfiguration in replicated databases based on group communication. In *Proc. Int. Conf. on Dependable Systems and Networks*, pages 117–130, 2001. DOI: 10.1109/DSN.2001.941398 116

B. Kemme, F. Pedone, G. Alonso, A. Schiper, and M. Wiesmann. Using optimistic atomic broadcast in transaction processing systems. *IEEE Trans. Knowl. and Data Eng.*, 15(4):1018–1032, 2003. DOI: 10.1109/TKDE.2003.1209016 64

A.-M. Kermarrec, A. I. T. Rowstron, M. Shapiro, and P. Druschel. The IceCube approach to the reconciliation of divergent replicas. In *Proc. ACM SIGACT-SIGOPS 20th Symp. on the Principles of Distributed Computing*, pages 210–218, 2001. DOI: 10.1145/383962.384020 17

J. J. Kistler and M. Satyanarayanan. Disconnected operation in the Coda file system. *ACM Trans. Comp. Syst.*, 10(1):3–25, 1992. DOI: 10.1145/146941.146942 102

K. Krikellas, S. Elnikety, Z. Vagena, and O. Hodson. Strongly consistent replication for a bargain. In *Proc. 25th Int. Conf. on Data Engineering*, pages 52–63, 2010. DOI: 10.1109/ICDE.2010.5447893 87

N. Krishnakumar and A. J. Bernstein. Bounded ignorance in replicated systems. In *Proc. 10th ACM SIGACT-SIGMOD-SIGART Symp. on Principles of Database Systems*, pages 63–74, 1991. DOI: 10.1145/113413.113419 101

H. T. Kung and J. T. Robinson. On optimistic methods for concurrency control. *ACM Trans. Database Syst.*, 6(2):213–226, 1981. DOI: 10.1145/319566.319567 86

E. Lau and S. Madden. An integrated approach to recovery and high availability in an updatable, distributed data warehouse. In *Proc. 32nd Int. Conf. on Very Large Data Bases*, pages 703–714, 2006. 116

W. Liang and B. Kemme. Online recovery in cluster databases. In *Advances in Database Technology, Proc. 11th Int. Conf. on Extending Database Technology*, pages 121–132, 2008. DOI: 10.1145/1353343.1353362 116

Y. Lin, B. Kemme, M. Patiño-Martínez, and R. Jiménez-Peris. Middleware based data replication providing snapshot isolation. In *Proc. ACM SIGMOD Int. Conf. on Management of Data*, pages 419–430, 2005. DOI: 10.1145/1066157.1066205 45, 87

Y. Lin, B. Kemme, M. Patiño-Martínez, and R. Jiménez-Peris. Enhancing edge computing with database replication. In *Proc. 26th Symp. on Reliable Distributed Systems*, pages 45–54, 2007. DOI: 10.1109/SRDS.2007.10 51

Y. Lin, B. Kemme, R. Jiménez-Peris, M. Patiño-Martínez, and J. E. Armendáriz-Iñigo. Snapshot isolation and integrity constraints in replicated databases. *ACM Trans. Database Syst.*, 34(2):Paper 11, 2009. DOI: 10.1145/1538909.1538913 15, 87

D. Malkhi and D. B. Terry. Concise version vectors in WinFS. *Distributed Computing*, 20(3): 209–219, 2007. DOI: 10.1007/s00446-007-0044-y 16, 102

K. Manassiev and C. Amza. Scaling and continuous availability in database server clusters through multiversion replication. In *Proc. Int. Conf. on Dependable Systems and Networks*, pages 666–676, 2007. DOI: 10.1109/DSN.2007.86 116

K. Manassiev, M. Mihailescu, and C. Amza. Exploiting distributed version concurrency in a transactional memory cluster. In *Proc. 11th ACM SIGPLAN Symp. on Principles and Practice of Parallel Programming*, pages 198–208, 2006. DOI: 10.1145/1122971.1123002 45

F. Mattern. Time and global states in distributed systems. In *Proc. of the Int. Workshop on Parallel and Distributed Algorithms*, 1989. 97

J. Milán, R. Jiménez-Peris, M. Patiño-Martínez, and B. Kemme. Adaptive middleware for data replication. In *Proc. ACM/IFIP/USENIX Int. Middleware Conf.*, pages 175–194, 2004. 117

H. Miranda, A. Pinto, and L. Rodrigues. Appia, a flexible protocol kernel supporting multiple coordinated channels. In *Proc. 21st Int. Conf. on Distributed Computing Systems*, pages 707–710, 2001. DOI: 10.1109/ICDSC.2001.919005 46

T. Mishima and H. Nakamura. Pangea: An eager database replication middleware guaranteeing snapshot isolation without modification of database servers. *PVLDB*, 2(1):1066–1077, 2009. 87

L. E. Moser, P. M. Melliar-Smith, D. A. Agarwal, R. K. Budhia, and C. A. Lingley-Papadopoulos. Totem: A fault-tolerant multicast group communication system. *Commun. ACM*, 39(4):54–63, 1996. DOI: 10.1145/227210.227226 46

F. D. Muñoz-Escoí, J. M. Bernabé-Gisbert, R. de Juan-Marín, J. E. Armendáriz-Iñigo, and J. R. González de Mendívil. Revising 1-copy equivalence in replicated databases with snapshot isolation. In *Proc. OTM Confederated Int. Conf. CoopIS, DOA, GADA, and ODBASE*, pages 467–483, 2009. DOI: 10.1007/978-3-642-05148-7_36 87

M. Nicola and M. Jarke. Performance modeling of distributed and replicated databases. *IEEE Trans. Knowl. and Data Eng.*, 12(4):645–672, 2000. DOI: 10.1109/69.868912 46, 52

Ch. Olston, B. Thau Loo, and J. Widom.   Adaptive precision setting for cached approximate values.   In *Proc. ACM SIGMOD Int. Conf. on Management of Data*, pages 355–366, 2001. DOI: 10.1145/376284.375710 101

M. T. Özsu and P. Valduriez. *Principles of Distributed Database Systems*. Prentice Hall, 1999. 127

E. Pacitti and E. Simon. Update propagation strategies to improve freshness in lazy master replicated databases. *VLDB J.*, 8(3-4):305–318, 2000. DOI: 10.1007/s007780050010 101

E. Pacitti, P. Minet, and E. Simon. Fast algorithm for maintaining replica consistency in lazy master replicated databases. In *Proc. 25th Int. Conf. on Very Large Data Bases*, pages 126–137, 1999. 102

E. Pacitti, C. Coulon, P. Valduriez, and M. T. Özsu.   Preventive replication in a database cluster. *Distributed and Parallel Databases*, 18(3):223–251, 2005. DOI: 10.1007/s10619-005-4257-4 46

M. Patiño-Martínez, R. Jiménez-Peris, B. Kemme, and G. Alonso.   MIDDLE-R: Consistent database replication at the middleware level.   *ACM Trans. Comp. Syst.*, 23(4):375–423, 2005. DOI: 10.1145/1113574.1113576 45, 64, 65

F. Pedone, R. Guerraoui, and A. Schiper. The database state machine approach. *Distributed and Parallel Databases*, 14(1):71–98, 2003. DOI: 10.1023/A:1022887812188 64

F. Perez-Sorrosal, M. Patiño-Martínez, R. Jiménez-Peris, and B. Kemme.   Consistent and scalable cache replication for multi-tier J2EE applications. In *Proc. ACM/IFIP/USENIX 8th Int. Middleware Conf.*, pages 328–347, 2007. DOI: 10.1007/978-3-540-76778-7_17 87, 120

Ch. Plattner and G. Alonso. Ganymed: Scalable replication for transactional web applications. In *Proc. ACM/IFIP/USENIX Int. Middleware Conf.*, pages 155–174, 2004. 45, 86

Ch. Plattner, G. Alonso, and M. T. Özsu.   DBFarm: A scalable cluster for multiple databases. In *Proc. ACM/IFIP/USENIX 7th Int. Middleware Conf.*, pages 180–200, 2006a. DOI: 10.1007/11925071_10 45

Ch. Plattner, G. Alonso, and M. T.-Özsu. Extending DBMSs with satellite databases. *VLDB J.*, 17 (4):657–682, 2006b. DOI: 10.1007/s00778-006-0026-x 45, 101

PostgreSQL. PostgreSQL, the world's most advanced open source database, 2007. http://www.postgresql.org; accessed on August, 15, 2010. 34

N. M. Preguiça, R. Rodrigues, C. Honorato, and J. Lourenço. Byzantium: Byzantine-fault-tolerant database replication providing snapshot isolation. In *Proc. of the 4th Workshop on Hot Topics in Systems Dependability (HotDep)*, 2008. 116

C. Pu and A. Leff. Replica control in distributed systems: An asynchronous approach. In *Proc. ACM SIGMOD Int. Conf. on Management of Data*, pages 377–386, 1991. DOI: 10.1145/119995.115856 101

M. Rabinovich, N. H. Gehani, and A. Kononov. Scalable update propagation in epidemic replicated databases. In *Advances in Database Technology, Proc. 5th Int. Conf. on Extending Database Technology*, pages 207–222, 1996. DOI: 10.1007/BFb0014154 102

U. Röhm, K. Böhm, and H.-J. Schek. OLAP query routing and physical design in a database cluster. In *Advances in Database Technology, Proc. 7th Int. Conf. on Extending Database Technology*, pages 254–268, 2000. DOI: 10.1007/3-540-46439-5_18 117

U. Röhm, K. Böhm, H.-J. Schek, and H. Schuldt. FAS - a freshness-sensitive coordination middleware for a cluster of OLAP components. In *Proc. 28th Int. Conf. on Very Large Data Bases*, pages 754–765, 2002. DOI: 10.1016/B978-155860869-6/50072-X 45, 101, 117

Y. Saito and M. Shapiro. Optimistic replication. *ACM Comp. Surv.*, 37(1):42–81, 2005. DOI: 10.1145/1057977.1057980 16, 102

J. Salas, R. Jiménez-Peris, M. Patiño-Martínez, and B. Kemme. Lightweight reflection for middleware-based database replication. In *Proc. 25th Symp. on Reliable Distributed Systems*, pages 377–390, 2006. DOI: 10.1109/SRDS.2006.28 45

N. Schiper, R. Schmidt, and F. Pedone. Optimistic algorithms for partial database replication. In *Proc. of Int. Conf. On Principles of DIstributed Systems*, pages 81–93, 2006. DOI: 10.1007/11945529_7 46

F. B. Schneider. Implementing fault-tolerant services using the state machine approach: A tutorial. *ACM Comp. Surv.*, 22(4):299–319, 1990. DOI: 10.1145/98163.98167 33

B. Schroeder, M. Harchol-Balter, A. Iyengar, E. M. Nahum, and A. Wierman. How to determine a good multi-programming level for external scheduling. In *Proc. 22nd Int. Conf. on Data Engineering*, page 60, 2006. DOI: 10.1109/ICDE.2006.78 117

D. Serrano, M. Patiño-Martínez, R. Jiménez, and B. Kemme. Boosting database replication scalability through partial replication and 1-copy-SI. In *Proc. of IEEE Pacific-Rim Conf. on Distributed Computing*, pages 290–297, 2007. 46, 52, 87

D. Serrano, M. Patiño-Martínez, R. Jiménez-Peris, and B. Kemme. An autonomic approach for replication of internet-based services. In *Proc. 27th Symp. on Reliable Distributed Systems*, pages 127–136, 2008. DOI: 10.1109/SRDS.2008.22 45, 46, 117

G. Soundararajan and C. Amza. Reactive provisioning of backend databases in shared dynamic content server clusters. *ACM Trans. on Autonomous and Adaptive Systems*, 1(2):151–188, 2006. DOI: 10.1145/1186778.1186780 117

G. Soundararajan, C. Amza, and A. Goel. Database replication policies for dynamic content applications. In *Proc. 1st ACM SIGOPS/EuroSys European Conf. on Computer Systems*, pages 89–102. ACM, 2006. DOI: 10.1145/1217935.1217945 117

A. Sousa, R. Oliveira, F. Moura, and F. Pedone.   Partial replication in the database state machine. In *Proc. IEEE Int. Symp. on Networking Computing and Applications*, pages 298–309, 2001. DOI: 10.1109/NCA.2001.962546 46

Spread. The Spread toolkit. http://www.spread.org; accessed on August, 15, 2010, 2007. 46

I. Stanoi, D. Agrawal, and A. El Abbadi.   Using broadcast primitives in replicated databases. In *Proc. 18th Int. Conf. on Distributed Computing Systems*, pages 148–155, 1998. DOI: 10.1109/ICDCS.1998.679497 64

D. B. Terry.   *Replicated Data Management for Mobile Computing.*   Morgan & Claypool, 2008.   Synthesis Lectures on Mobile and Pervasive Computing. DOI: 10.2200/S00132ED1V01Y200807MPC005 121

D. B. Terry, M. Theimer, K. Petersen, A. J. Demers, M. Spreitzer, and C. Hauser. Managing update conflicts in Bayou, a weakly connected replicated storage system. In *Proc. 15th ACM Symp. on Operating System Principles*, pages 172–183, 1995. DOI: 10.1145/224057.224070 102

R. van Renesse, K. P. Birman, and S. Maffeis. Horus: A flexible group communication system. *Commun. ACM*, 39(4):76–83, 1996. DOI: 10.1145/227210.227229 46

B. Vandiver, H. Balakrishnan, B. Liskov, and S. Madden. Tolerating byzantine faults in transaction processing systems using commit barrier scheduling. In *Proc. 21st ACM Symp. on Operating System Principles*, pages 59–72, 2007. 104, 116

R. Vilaça, J. Pereira, R. Oliveira, J.E. Armendariz, and J.R. Gonzalez. On the cost of database clusters reconfiguration. In *Proc. 28th Symp. on Reliable Distributed Systems*, pages 259–267, 2009. DOI: 10.1109/SRDS.2009.27 116

W. Vogels. Eventually consistent. *ACM Queue*, 6(6):14–19, 2008. DOI: 10.1145/1466443.1466448 16

W. Wang and C. Amza. On optimal concurrency control for optimistic replication. In *Proc. 24rd Int. Conf. on Distributed Computing Systems*, pages 317–326, 2009. DOI: 10.1109/ICDCS.2009.71 102

M. Wiesmann and A. Schiper.   Comparison of database replication techniques based on total order broadcast.   *IEEE Trans. Knowl. and Data Eng.*, 17(4):551–566, 2005. DOI: 10.1109/TKDE.2005.54 52

O. Wolfson, S. Jajodia, and Y. Huang. An adaptive data replication algorithm. *ACM Trans. Database Syst.*, 22(2):255–314, 1997. DOI: 10.1145/249978.249982 46, 117

S. Wu and B. Kemme. Postgres-R(SI): Combining replica control with concurrency control based on snapshot isolation. In *Proc. 21st Int. Conf. on Data Engineering*, pages 422–433, 2005. 45, 46, 86

H. Yu and A. Vahdat. Design and evaluation of a conit-based continuous consistency model for replicated services. *ACM Trans. Comp. Syst.*, 20(3):239–282, 2002. DOI: 10.1145/566340.566342 101

V. Zuikeviciute and F. Pedone. Conflict-aware load-balancing techniques for database replication. In *Proc. 2008 ACM Symp. on Applied Computing*, pages 2169–2173, 2008. DOI: 10.1145/1363686.1364205 117

Authors' Biographies

BETTINA KEMME

Bettina Kemme is associate professor at the School of Computer Science of McGill University, Montreal, Canada. She received her undergraduate degree at the Friedrich-Alexander University in Erlangen, Germany, and her Ph.D. at the Swiss Federal Institute of Technology in Zurich (ETHZ). Her research focus lies in the design and development of distributed information systems, in particular, in data consistency aspects and the interplay between communication and data management. Her work on data replication is well known in the database and distributed systems communities. She has been PC member of many database and distributed systems conferences, such as VLDB, SIGMOD, ICDE, EDBT, Middleware, ICDCS, Eurosys, and P2P. She has been on the Editorial Board for the Encyclopedia of Database Systems, Springer, and track co-chair of ICDE 2009. She is area editor of Information Systems, Elsevier.

RICARDO JIMÉNEZ PERIS

Ricardo Jiménez Peris is associate professor at Universidad Politecnica de Madrid and co-director of the Distributed Systems Lab (LSD). He received his master and PhD degrees from Universidad Politecnica de Madrid. He was a visiting postdoc researcher at the Swiss Federal Institute of Technology in Zurich (ETHZ). His research interests have been around scalable and fault tolerant distributed systems and currently focusing on cloud computing. His research on scalable data replication during the last decade has obtained well-known results in the distributed systems and database communities. He is coordinator of the Stream European project on data stream cloud systems. He has served as General chair at SRDS, Programme committee chair at EDCC, workshop chair at ICDCS, and tutorial chair at LADC, as well as Programme committee member at ICDCS, DSN, DISC, SRDS, EDCC among others. He has also been member of the expert group on cloud computing appointed by the European Commission.

MARTA PATIÑO-MARTÍNEZ

Marta Patiño-Martínez is associate professor at the Computer Science School of Universidad Politecnica de Madrid, Madrid, Spain. She received her master degree from Universidad Politecnica de Valencia, Spain and her PhD degree from Universidad Politecnica de Madrid. She was a visiting postdoc researcher at the Swiss Federal Institute of Technology in Zurich (ETHZ). Her research has focused on distributed systems with special emphasis on scalability and high availability. Her research on scalable data replication during the last 10 years has attracted the attention of many researchers from the distributed systems and database community. She is coordinator of the CumuloNimbo European project on cloud transactional systems. She has served in the Programme Committee of several distributed and database conferences such as VLDB, ICDCS, ICDE, SRDS, Middleware, and EDCC.